The Old Farmer's ALMANAC for Kids

VOLUME 5

YANKEE PUBLISHING
INCORPORATED

The Old Farmer's Almanac **Books**

Publisher: Sherin Pierce

Series editor: Janice Stillman
Art director: Margo Letourneau
Copy editor: Jack Burnett
Contributors: Jack Burnett, Alice Cary, Gregory Danner, Martha Deeringer, Mare-Anne Jarvela, Martie Majoros, Amy Nieskens, Sarah Perreault, Montana Rogers, Jessie Salisbury, Heidi Stonehill, Sophia Yin

V.P., new media and production: Paul Belliveau
Production directors: Susan Gross, David Ziarnowski
Production artists: Lucille Rines, Rachel Kipka, Janet Grant

Companion Web site: Almanac4kids.com

Web editor: Catherine Boeckmann
Web designers: Lou S. Eastman, Amy O'Brien
E-commerce manager: Alan Henning
Programming: Reinvented, Inc.

For additional information about this and other publications from *The Old Farmer's Almanac,* visit **Almanac.com** or call **800-ALMANAC** (800-256-2622)

Consumer marketing manager: Kate McPherson

Distributed in the book trade in the United States by Houghton Mifflin Harcourt and in Canada by Thomas Allen & Son Limited

Direct-to-retail and bulk sales are handled by Cindy Schlosser, 800-895-9265, ext. 126, or Stacey Korpi, ext. 160

Yankee Publishing Inc., P.O. Box 520, 1121 Main Street, Dublin, New Hampshire 03444

ISBN: 978-1-57198-613-9
ISSN: 1948-061X

FIRST PRINTING OF VOLUME 5

Thank you to everyone who had a hand in producing this Almanac and getting it to market, including printers, distributors, and sales and delivery people.

PRINTED IN THE UNITED STATES OF AMERICA

Hey, Kids!

WELCOME to the latest edition of **The Old Farmer's Almanac for Kids!**

If you like to read, to cook or just eat, to grow things or take care of animals, to gaze at the night sky, to run sack races or jump frogs, to explore swamps or listen for howling wolves, to dance, to geocache, to do puzzles and solve riddles, to predict the weather, or to surf, ski, or juggle, this book has something for you—and this is not everything that you'll find in here!

Even if you read this book from cover to cover, every time you open it you'll come across something that you didn't know or something that you want to do. Promise!

Whether this is the first **Old Farmer's Almanac for Kids** volume that you read or the fifth, we hope that you'll find it fascinating and well worth sharing with your friends and family.

From each and every one of us to each and every one of you . . . **have fun!**

The Editors

➡️ **P.S.** When you have a chance, please go to **Almanac4kids.com/TellUs** (or mail a letter to us at P.O. Box 520, Dublin, NH 03444) and let us know what you think about this book. What do you like best? (Parents, and teachers, we'd love to hear from you, too.) Thanks, everybody!

CONTENTS

40

Calendar

Astronomy

Weather

Nature

8

62

100

68

118

85

(continued on next page) ➡

CONTENTS

(continued)

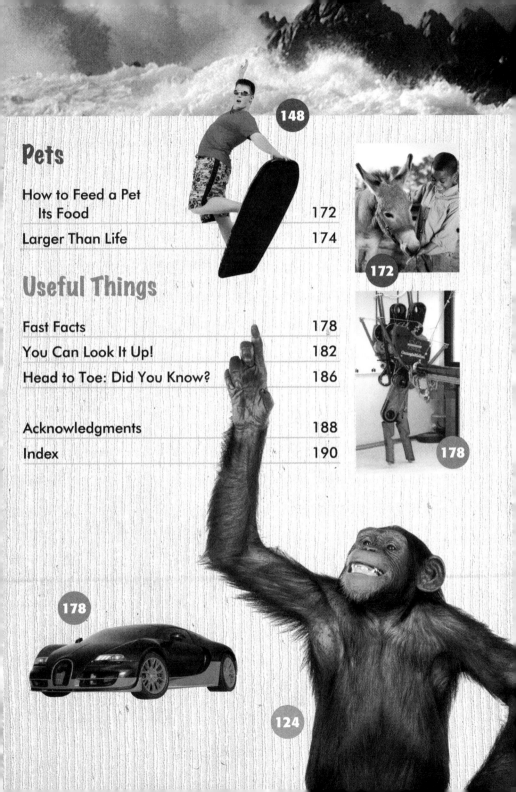

Pets

Useful Things

Make ⇒ EVERY Day

JANUARY

We all celebrate certain days with traditional foods and customary festivities. Think of
⇒ your birthday
⇒ Halloween
⇒ Christmas
⇒ Chanukah
⇒ Valentine's Day
and lots more. But almost every day—or week or month—is *special!* Here are a few of those "other" days, with ideas for fun activities. (If these activities don't fit into your calendar on their day, do them when you have time!)

INTERNATIONAL WAYFINDING MONTH

⇒ **Visit a museum, a mall, an airport, or a city** or take a walk around your town or school and notice the ways in which directions are presented for walking, cycling, driving, and/or other modes of travel (wheelchair, stroller, skateboard, horse). What words are used? What symbols? Choose two locations that are convenient to you. Develop a map and make signage to get people from one location to the other and back. Or create teams and develop maps and signage for several locations. Test the maps with friends or family and write a report on how well they work.

January 1

DISHONOR DAY

On this day, ever since **1976,** Lake Superior State University in Sault Ste. Marie, Michigan, has issued a list of overused words and phrases. Past lists have included the words *amazing, ginormous, viral* (referring to spreading information on the Internet), and *sweet.* Make a list of words that you hear or use that you think should be banished, then make a list of words to use instead. Share these with other kids at **Almanac4kids.com/TellUs.**

NOTE PAD

Words that should be banished!
1.
2.
3.
4.
5.
6.

January 17

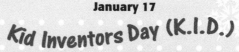

Kid Inventors Day (K.I.D.)

January 17 is the birthday of **Benjamin Franklin,** one of America's youngest inventors. Franklin made swim flippers from wood when he was 11 years old! What can you invent? An invention can be a new product or process that fills a need, solves a problem, or makes life easier or more fun. Research kid inventors and things they have done. Then, identify an object to reinvent (a backpack, for example). Make a list of the problems with backpacks. List ways to eliminate the problems and improvements to make. Draw a sketch of your new backpack (or other object). Finally, invent a new name for it.

continued ⇨

NATIONAL
BIRDFEEDING
Month (U.S.)

Make a feeder. Remove the label from a clean, dry, 2-liter soda bottle with cap. Tie a piece of cord or wire around the neck of the bottle so that you will be able to hang the feeder. Make perches for the birds by drilling holes in opposite sides of the bottle and pushing small dowels all the way through. If necessary, seal the holes around the dowels with hot glue. *(Ask an adult to help.)* Drill small holes an inch or two above each perch so that the birds can peck and get the seeds. Fill the bottle with birdseed and screw on the bottle cap. Hang your feeder and watch the birds that visit it.

SWEET

Sweet potatoes are grown from slips— sprouts that develop their own roots. Most varieties require long growing seasons. If you live in the north, try 'Centennial', which needs 90 to 100 days to mature.

You can buy sweet potato slips from garden centers, nurseries, or local farmers. Or, to grow your own:

1 Go to your supermarket and **select untreated sweet potatoes** with no blemishes or cracks. One potato should yield about 12 slips.

2 **Store the sweet potatoes** in a well-lit room with a temperature between 70° and 80°F. Place them in a box about 2 inches apart and 2 inches deep in a good-quality potting soil. Water regularly to prevent them from drying out. Do not overwater. In 2 to 4 weeks, you should see sprouts (the slips) growing up past the soil.

POTATO

month

3 When the slips are 6 to 12 inches tall and all danger of frost has passed, carefully remove them from the potato and **plant them outdoors** in fertile, well-tilled, well-drained soil deep enough to cover their roots and about ½ inch of the stem. Set them 12 to 18 inches apart.

4 **Water the slips** generously for a few days to make sure that the plants root well. Water regularly thereafter.

5 **Fertilize** with a 5-10-10 mix 3 to 4 weeks after transplanting.

6 **Weed occasionally.** Do not prune the vines.

Harvest 3 to 4 months after planting, when the leaves begin to yellow.

MAKE SWEET POTATO CHIPS

Preheat the oven to 350°F. Peel two sweet potatoes and slice thin. *(Ask an adult to help.)* Cover a cookie sheet with foil and spray it lightly with vegetable oil spray. Arrange the sweet potatoes on the prepared sheet, then lightly spray the tops of the potatoes with oil and sprinkle lightly with salt, if desired. Bake for 20 minutes, turn them over, sprinkle the other side with salt, if desired, and bake for 10 minutes more.

continued ⇨

February 2
Groundhog Day

According to folklore, if a groundhog sees his shadow at sunrise today, winter weather will continue for 6 more weeks. Research this tradition, including the events in Punxsutawney, Pennsylvania, and Wiarton, Ontario. Draw a comic strip to tell the story.

February 15
Anniversary of Canada's
MAPLE LEAF FLAG

➡ On this day in 1965, the red and white flag with the red maple leaf in the center was first raised at Ottawa, Ontario.

🍁 **Research the National Flag of Canada.** Think about your family and its history. Design a flag to represent your family history.

First full week in March:

M A R C H ➡ Celebrate Your NAME Week

Your name identifies you to the world. It is who you are, so have fun with it!

⬇

Research the most popular baby names for your birth year. Then research the popularity of *your* name. Make a chart showing how your name ranks over time.

⬇

Research your family tree and note the names of members of each generation. Look up the origin and meanings of the names. Create a new family tree (or list) from this information and share it with your family.

⬇

Using the first letters of your name(s), find words to describe yourself. For example, M = mysterious; **A** = artistic; **R** = runner; **C** = courageous.

⬇

Learn the song "The Name Game." Insert the names of you and your friends or family and make rhymes that fit the beat.

🍁 **Conduct a "blind" maple syrup tasting** (include an artificial version), with participants commenting on and rating the samples.

🍁 **Attend a maple sugaring event** and see sap turned into syrup or make fake maple syrup (see below). Write a report that compares the processes.

YOU WILL NEED:

1 cup water
2 cups sugar
maple extract
   flavoring,
   to taste

Put the water and sugar into a pan. Cook on medium heat until the sugar is dissolved, stirring occasionally. Add maple flavoring, to taste. Serve on pancakes and waffles.

March is

Music in Our Schools Month

Think you have no musical talent? Line up some empty glass bottles. Partially fill them with different amounts of water. Push your upper lip out over your lower one and blow straight down into each bottle until you hear a musical tone. What do you notice about the pitches made by the different bottles? Use your bottles to play a tune. Gather more bottles and a few friends and create a bottle band. Perform a familiar tune for your class. Can they guess it?

March 31

Anniversary of the Eiffel Tower

On this day in 1889, the Eiffel Tower was dedicated in Paris, France. The ceremony was presided over by the tower's designer and namesake, GUSTAVE EIFFEL. What landmarks have you visited? Do you know how they got their names? Design a statue, landmark, or sculpture and name it after someone you know. Gather your friends and family and present your project. Explain how your design represents the person for whom it is named.

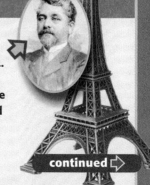

continued ▷

April

Any day in April:

Library SNAPSHOT Day(s)

Show the many ways in which people use your library in a single day! With the librarian's permission, interview library patrons about how they use the library. Take pictures (or videos) of these activities. Arrange the pictures on a poster, with the stories, to display in the library. Or edit the video and then arrange and publicize a time to show it to patrons.

April 22

EARTH DAY

Improve Earth by making earth: Turn garbage and other "stuff" into compost! Research how to start and maintain a compost pile, make a list of the good and bad and "green" and "brown" ingredients. Find a suitable place for the pile in your yard and begin. Record the date when you add certain items (banana skins, eggshells, shredded newspaper) and track how long it takes for these items to break down. Occasionally, put a compost thermometer inside the pile and compare the warmth of the air to the decomposing matter. Why is there a greater difference in temperature at certain times?

Richter Scale Day

On this day in 1900, writer, physicist, and seismologist Charles Francis Richter was born. He invented the Richter Scale for measuring earthquake magnitude. Today, scientists use the Moment Magnitude Scale. Research and compare the two scales. Earthquakes occur somewhere in the world almost every day! See where and exactly when, as well as the magnitude, at **Earthquake.usgs.gov.**

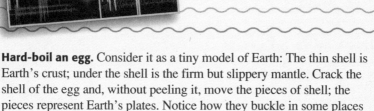

Hard-boil an egg. Consider it as a tiny model of Earth: The thin shell is Earth's crust; under the shell is the firm but slippery mantle. Crack the shell of the egg and, without peeling it, move the pieces of shell; the pieces represent Earth's plates. Notice how they buckle in some places and expose "mantle" in other places. On Earth's surface, the same type of activity results in the formation of mountains, earthquakes, and new ocean floor.

continued ⇨

M A Y

NATIONAL BIKE MONTH (U.S.)

Research the rules of the road for cyclists. Then, set up an obstacle course for bicycles. (Be sure to wear your helmet and elbow and knee pads!) Place garbage cans, laundry baskets, lawn chairs, a wheelbarrow, and other obstacles on a playground or grassy field. Draw a map to show your friends the route they should ride around the obstacles. Compete to see who can ride the course without running into any obstacles. Use a stopwatch to measure the fastest time.

May 12

Limerick Day

Today is the birthday of Edward Lear, who published *A Book of Nonsense* in 1846. With it, Lear popularized the limerick, a five-line poem with a specific rhyme scheme. Here's an example:

There once was an ape in a zoo

Who often asked "How do you do?"

Of surprised passersby

Until one made reply:

"I'm fine, sir—how is it with you?"

Now, write a limerick that begins with

There once was a flea on a dog . . .

HAVING FUN?

Write limericks about another animal, a vacation, a family member, or a historical figure. Share these with other kids at Almanac4kids.com/TellUs.

May 25

National

TAP DANCE

Day
(U.S.)

Celebrate tap dancing as an art form on the anniversary of the birth of Bill "Bojangles" Robinson, who famously danced with child actress Shirley Temple. In the 1935 film *The Little Colonel,* he teaches Shirley Temple's character how to dance up the stairs. Find videos of the national anthem of tap—the "Shim Sham" (or "Shim Sham Shimmy"). Gather a few friends and learn the dance. You don't need taps on your shoes to do it.

JUNE

National

DAIRY MONTH
(U.S.)

Make butter! Put some heavy cream in a clean glass jar and seal it tightly with a lid. Shake, shake, and shake some more. After about 10 minutes, you'll see a solid in the jar. This is the butter. The liquid that is left over is the buttermilk. Use the butter on toast and drink the buttermilk or use it to make pancakes.

continued ⇨

First Saturday in June:

National Trails Day
(U.S.)

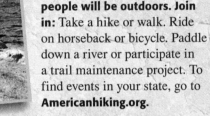

⬤ **On this day, thousands of people will be outdoors. Join in:** Take a hike or walk. Ride on horseback or bicycle. Paddle down a river or participate in a trail maintenance project. To find events in your state, go to **Americanhiking.org**.

⬤ **Step back in time: Research the routes that 18th- and 19th-century pioneers followed** as they moved westward across America—in particular, the California, Oregon, Santa Fe, Mormon, Applegate, Gila, Bozeman, and Denver trails. Trace each trail on a large, modern-day road map of the United States. What are the differences between the trails and the map's modern highways?

June 8

World Oceans

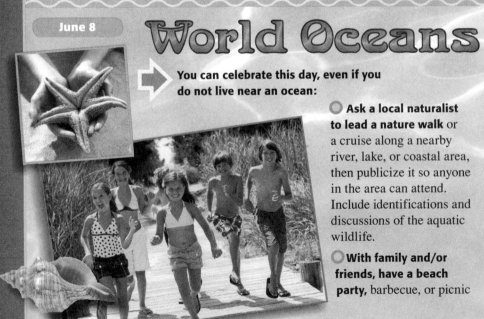

➡ **You can celebrate this day, even if you do not live near an ocean:**

⬤ **Ask a local naturalist to lead a nature walk** or a cruise along a nearby river, lake, or coastal area, then publicize it so anyone in the area can attend. Include identifications and discussions of the aquatic wildlife.

⬤ **With family and/or friends, have a beach party,** barbecue, or picnic

June 14

National Flag Day

(U.S.)

Research national flag history and etiquette and present the information to a class in a school grade below your own. Have an essay contest: Ask students to write about what the flag means to them. Make arrangements for the best essayists to raise and lower the flag at school.

Day

with contests for best sea creature costume and/or sand castle. Dance to music such as "Catch a Wave" and "Surfin' U.S.A."

○ **Check with your local aquarium** to see if they offer sleepovers. You'll learn about what ocean creatures do at night.

continued ⇨

National
HORSERADISH
Month (U.S.)

➡️ **Research horseradish: Where does it get its name?** What is it? How does it grow? What makes it "hot"? Buy a fresh piece of thick, fleshy, white horseradish root, and prepare it to eat: Peel the root and cut it into cubes for about 1 cup. Put the horseradish cubes into a blender. Add one or two ice cubes and grind the horseradish until smooth.

(Make sure that you do this in a well-ventilated room. The smell will be quite pungent.) For mild horseradish, add 1 to 2 tablespoons of white vinegar and a few pinches of salt immediately. For hot and spicy horseradish, wait 3 minutes before adding 1 to 2 tablespoons of white vinegar and a few pinches of salt. Serve with meat or make a horseradish sandwich.

HORSERADISH & PB SANDWICH

2 slices whole wheat bread	2 teaspoons prepared horseradish
2 tablespoons mayonnaise	2 tablespoons peanut butter

● Toast the bread. Combine the mayonnaise and horseradish in a small bowl. Spread peanut butter on one slice of bread. Spread the horseradish mixture on the other slice of bread. Put one piece of bread on top of the other. Slice and eat.

Third Saturday in July:

CANADA'S

T housands of people participate in fun, educational, family-oriented events in parks and historic sites across Canada.

Past programs have included lumberjack competitions and demonstrations; wildflower walks and eco-challenge

▶ **July 22: Spooner's Day**

A spoonerism, named for **REVEREND ARCHIBALD SPOONER,** who was born on this day in 1844, is a switch of letters or sounds in words so that they come out differently than they should. This happened often to Reverend Spooner.

PARKS DAY

Fourth Saturday
in July:
National Day of the

Cowboy
(U.S.)

21

C A L E N D A R

hikes; traditional
Aboriginal food,
crafts, music, and
storytelling;
campfires with
interpretation,
songs, and skits; and
kite-making workshops. Check the events page at
Parksday.ca for activities near you.

The Pro Rodeo Hall
of Fame and Museum
of the American
Cowboy is in Colorado
Springs, Colorado. If
you can't go there in
person, visit the Web site
Prorodeohalloffame.com
and find out who is the
best of the best in rodeo.
Pick one of the rodeo
riders inducted into the
hall of fame and find out
everything you can about
him or her. Write a speech
that details the advice you
think that person would
give to young rodeo riders
today.

Examples are **"bunny phone"** (funny bone),
"Please sew me to another sheet"
(please show me to another seat),
and **"a well-boiled icicle"** (a
well-oiled bicycle). Sometimes
spoonerisms happen by accident,
but sometimes they are done
intentionally, for fun. Collect
spoonerisms and compile a
humorous dictionary titled
Tips of the Slongue. Share
these with other kids at
Almanac4kids.com/TellUs.

continued ⇨

August 13   I N T E R N A T I O N A L

LEFT-HANDERS' Day

Survey family or **friends who are lefties** (even if you are, too) and make a list of the difficulties that left-handed people experience doing everyday things. Based on your information, design a tool for a left-hander. Possibilities for new designs include scissors, a mug, a computer keyboard, a pencil sharpener, and a can opener. Make a drawing of your design or build a model.

Third Monday in August:

DISCOVERY DAYS

Yukon Territory, Canada

Around this time in 1896, three "sourdoughs"—George Carmack, Dawson Charlie, and Skookum Jim—found gold in a stream now known as Bonanza Creek. Their discovery set off one of the world's greatest gold rush stampedes.

▷ Prospectors in the western United States and Canada were called "sourdoughs" because sourdough bread was one of their main sources of food. Research why. With help from an adult, make sourdough bread or buy a loaf. How does it compare to regular yeast bread?

▷ Gold is hard to find these days, but "special" stones and items can be found in almost any river or pond—even the ocean. Use an old window screen or an aluminum pie plate with holes punched into the bottom, or make a "gold pan" by securing net material in a quilting hoop. Take it to the nearest waterfront and sift for treasures.

Third Saturday in August:

International Geocaching Day

Geocaching is a high-tech treasure-hunting game using GPS-enabled devices. It is played by people of all ages around the world. Letterboxing is a low-tech treasure-hunting game using a compass, ink and a personal stamp, and a waterproof container. Research both activities, then plan and execute a hunt, based on whichever game suits you best.

Saturday of last full weekend in August:

International **BAT NIGHT**

Bats are an important part of our ecosystem. Research why that is true, then . . .

- **Build a bat house.** To learn how, get directions at **Batconservation.org** and work with an adult.

- **Find the names of ten or more species** of bats. (Nearly a thousand are known!) Fit them into a crossword or word search puzzle or make them into anagrams.

- **Use black construction paper to make several bats.** Create a bat mobile to hang in your room.

continued ⇨

September

HAPPY CAT MONTH

➡ **We often speak of cats to describe our behavior.** For example, you can take a catnap; the cat can get your tongue; your brother is a copycat; getting friends together is like herding cats. Research to find more such phrases, then write a story using as many as you can.

Share it with other kids at **Almanac4kids.com/TellUs.**

If you have a cat, observe it on a regular basis for at least a month. In a notebook, record when, where, and for how long your cat purrs. What conclusions can you draw about what makes your cat purr or how purring benefits your pet?

National Chicken Month (U.S.)

⬤ **People have been playing with eggs perhaps since the first chicken laid one.** Research and then reenact popular egg games of the 19th century, including "Egg Picking," "Egg Ball," and "Egg Croquet."

⬤ **Save the bones from a roast chicken dinner.** Boil them and remove all of the meat. Soak the bones for 2 to 3 days in vinegar. They will get soft. Dry them thoroughly. Then use fishing line to tie the bones back together into a real chicken skeleton!

Last Saturday in September:

National Public Lands Day (U.S.)

Lend a hand (or two!). Join thousands of volunteers across the country. Contact a park or other public space near you and offer to help clean up, build trails or bridges, plant trees, weed— or whatever is needed. Enlist family or friends and do it as a team.

Week containing 10th day of the 10th month:

National
METRIC
Week (U.S.)

Fourth week in October:

National Chemistry Week
(U.S.)

- **Make a metric "body ruler,"** based on specific parts of your body. Using a metric ruler, measure your hand span (from the tip of your thumb to the tip of your baby finger, with hand outstretched), the length of your forearm, and the length of your foot. Using these "body rulers," estimate the sizes of other things— books, pencils, desks, etc.

- In the school cafeteria, **post signs that identify the portion sizes of food items,** including beverages, in both metric units and standard measures.

- **Make a map of your school** or home using metric units and post it in a prominent place.

Some fruit and vegetables are natural batteries: They generate a slight electrical charge. You can make a battery from a potato or a lemon.

Insert a galvanized (zinc-coated) nail in one spot. Insert a thick copper wire in another. Set an electrical tester (voltmeter) at its lowest voltage range and touch its probes to the nail and the wire.

You may detect a slight current. Research the chemistry that accounts for this electrifying reaction.

continued ⇨

OCTOBER

(continued)

INTERNATIONAL Magic Week

Learn an illusion, such as how to make dirty "laundry" disappear.

YOU WILL NEED:

6 handkerchief-size pieces of white cloth

paint, markers, or food to stain the handkerchiefs

2 paper lunch bags of the same size

scissors

TO PREPARE:

Stain three of the handkerchiefs. Set them aside. Cut 2 inches from the top of one of the lunch bags. Fold three clean handkerchiefs, then place them in the bottom of the taller bag. Open the shorter bag inside the taller bag. Push the shorter bag down, so that only ¼ inch of it sticks out of the taller bag on every side. Roll over the tops of both bags together to make a folded rim.

Use magic words ("hocus-pocus," "abracadabra," and other phrases) as you perform the trick:

1. Show the audience the stained handkerchiefs.

2. Show the audience the inside of the "empty" bag.

3. Place the dirty handkerchiefs in the shorter bag.

4. Gather the neck of the bag as you would the neck of a bottle. Grasp it in a bunch.

5. Put the neck of the bag to your mouth and gently blow some air

into it to inflate it. Squeeze the neck of the bag with your thumb and forefinger (to keep the air in). Clap your other hand into the bottom of the bag(s) to "pop" it. The outer bag should rip, revealing the clean handkerchiefs "hidden" there.

6. Turn the ripped bag toward you and pull out the clean handkerchiefs. Bunch the bags tightly and toss them aside.

November 3

Anniversary of the adoption of

SOS

• • • ▬ ▬ ▬ • • •

On this day in 1906, the Second **International Radio Telegraphic Conference at Berlin, Germany, proposed a new distress signal: SOS.** It uses letters of Morse Code, a method of communicating in short and long sounds (expressed as dots and dashes on paper) used by telegraph and radio operators. Research **Samuel Morse,** the man who invented the code. Write a script for a one-act play in which Samuel Morse time-travels to the 21st century and sees how communications have changed.

November 11

National ORIGAMI Day (Japan)

Origami, which originated in Japan, is the ancient art of folding a square piece of paper into shapes and figures. Try it! Make a windmill (two-star difficulty):

1 fold in half to make a crease, then unfold

2 fold in both ends to meet at the center crease

3 fold top and bottom to meet in the center

4 unfold at top and bottom

5 open the corners, then fold forward at the dotted lines

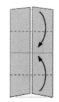

6 flatten the bottom crease and repeat step 5 for the top

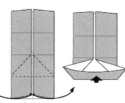

7 fold at the dotted line

8 open at the arrows slightly to make spaces

9 push a pin through the center of the windmill and into a straw or small stick

Explore En.origami-club.com and start now to make origami favors as gifts for friends for the upcoming holidays.

continued ⇨

November 19

Anniversary of the

GETTYSBURG ADDRESS

On this day in 1863, following the U.S. Civil War's Battle of Gettysburg (Pennsylvania), President Abraham Lincoln delivered one of the most famous speeches in the English language.

DECEMBER

National ## DAY OF THE HORSE (U.S.)

Second Saturday in December

Visit a stable and interview the groom about caring for horses. Write up a story for your school or community newspaper.

Find out why horseshoes are hung over doors for good luck. Write a short story in which a good luck horseshoe is important to the plot.

Gather friends and have a horse movie marathon, watching these films: *Black Beauty, Secretariat, Casey's Shadow, Flicka, National Velvet.*

The Gettysburg Address, which begins with "Four score and seven years ago . . . ," is only 273 words long and took Lincoln less than 2 minutes to give. Research a copy of the speech and memorize it, with the goal of reciting it in 2 minutes or less.

December 11

International MOUNTAIN Day

► **Identify the mountains in your state or region.** (If none exist near you, identify 12 around the world.) Research how they got their names. Once you find out, make a crossword puzzle of the names with clues.

► **Research famous people who have climbed the world's highest mountain, Everest:** the first person; the first woman; the youngest person; the oldest person; the first sightless person. Write a report on their trips, noting the differences in conditions, equipment, and other unique aspects of their treks.

Mt. Everest

_M_ ake this snack for a horse. *(Ask an adult for help.)*

Oat 'n' Carrot Cookies

1 cup old-fashioned oatmeal
1 cup flour
1 teaspoon salt
1 teaspoon sugar
1 cup chopped carrots
2 teaspoons vegetable oil
¼ cup molasses

Preheat the oven to 350°F and grease a cookie sheet. In a large bowl, combine the oatmeal, flour, salt, and sugar. Add the carrots, oil, and molasses and stir. Form the dough into small balls and place them on the sheet. Bake for 15 minutes, or until golden brown. Let cool and store in a tin. Makes 12 cookies.

December 14 through January 5

Christmas Bird Count

_P_ articipate in the annual Audubon Christmas Bird Count in your area. Founded by ornithologist Frank Chapman in 1900, this tradition is the longest-running wildlife census and has grown to include tens of thousands of volunteers throughout the Americas. Research to locate and contact your local Count Compiler to find out how you can volunteer for one day (that's all it takes!).

OVER THE

MOON

EXTRA! EXTRA! Read All About It!

In 1835, the publishers of *The New York Sun* newspaper wanted to sell more papers. So, on August 25, the first of a series of articles appeared claiming that British astronomer Sir John Herschel had used a gigantic telescope to discover life on the Moon. The reporter claimed that Herschel had seen blue unicorns, horned bears, beavers that walked on two feet, and humans with wings ("man-bats"), as well as sheep, zebras, pelicans, cranes, and other exotic creatures amid amethyst obelisks, volcanic mountains, and forests.

Readers were fascinated, and sales of the newspaper took off.

The articles ran for 6 days ending on August 31. Yet even before that

The MOON IN VIEW

Sir John Herschel

final account, people began asking why no other newspapers had reported the event. Some folks began to doubt the stories, but they enjoyed them all the same.

The articles became known as The Great Moon Hoax. No one at the newspaper ever admitted that the story was a fantasy, and the true identity of the writer was never revealed. Herschel, who was living in South Africa at the time, learned about the hoax months later.

Reports of the Moon's inhabitants described "man-bats," horned bears, and exotic creatures.

- We see the same side, or hemisphere, of the Moon all the time because Earth's gravity has slowed the Moon's rotation; now one Moon rotation and one Moon revolution around Earth take the same amount of time.

- The surface of the Moon may appear to be silvery gray, white, or pale yellow, but it is primarily charcoal gray. The presence of iron oxide creates reds, and titanium oxide introduces shades of blue. A full Moon may appear orange because Earth's atmosphere acts as a filter, minimizing the blues.

continued ➡

On the surface of the Moon in 1971, *Apollo 15* lunar module pilot Jim Irwin prepared the lunar rover for the first lunar ride.

▶ Moondust, also called lunar regolith, is retroreflective. Like a road sign, it reflects light back to the source (the Sun). Some sunlight rays bounce off the Moon and travel to Earth. During a full Moon, Earth is roughly in the same direction as the Sun, so it receives more reflected sunlight than at other times.

▶ Because the Moon reflects all light wavelengths and we most often view it at night against a black sky, it appears nearly white or yellowish most of the time.

DID YOU KNOW

Moonlight: a term that refers to holding a second job, usually at night ⬇

Moonflower: A member of the morning glory family, it blooms in the evening and usually closes by morning.

Moon jellyfish: Found in abundance in the mid-Atlantic Ocean, it has an 18-inch umbrella, or disc, that resembles a flying saucer.

COLOR CHECK

THE MOON'S

FULL NAMES

The celestial body that revolves around Earth has many names . . .

- The English word "moon" comes from the Old English *MONA*.

- In Italian, Latin, and Spanish, the orb is called *LUNA*, for the Roman Moon goddess.

- In French, the word for moon is *LUNE*.

- Germans use *MOND*.

- Celestial bodies that hold the same position around other planets as the Moon does around Earth are collectively called "moons."

Jupiter's largest moons: Io, Europa, Ganymede, and Callisto

 Get the date of the next full Moon at Almanac4kids.com/Sky. On the full Moon day, take a sheet of white paper and cut a hole in it about ¼ inch in diameter. On that night, look at the Moon through the hole, while holding the paper at arm's length and shining a white light on the paper. Now what color is the Moon? (The answer is below.)

Answer: dull gray

continued ➡

One Size Fits All

Sometimes when a full Moon sits low on the horizon, it appears to be enormous. Some people mistakenly believe that the full Moon appears large because our atmosphere magnifies our image of it. This is known as the "Moon illusion."

In fact, the Moon is not magnified nor does it change size:

► When the Moon is high overhead, it is dwarfed by the vast hemisphere of the heavens.

► When the Moon is low, it is viewed in proximity to earthly objects, such as chimneys or trees, the size and shape of which provide scale.

LUNAR LORE

Myths and legends about the Moon abound. While they are not scientific, they have a long and colorful history. Here are a few:

Build a fence when the Moon is setting, and the bottom rail will be buried in 3 years.

Plant corn when the Moon is rising, and you will have a very tall stalk with the ear hanging straight down the stalk so that no water can enter.

Plant potatoes when the Moon is setting, or the crop will be shallow and every potato will be badly sunburned.

Nails and hair grow faster if cut by the light of the Moon.

MOON

An artist's concept of a space tug docked with a lunar lander, orbiting Earth while preparing for its journey to the Moon's surface

Imagine that you are part of a space exploration mission flying from a space station orbiting the Moon to an occupied base on the Moon itself. An instrument malfunction causes you to crash on the Moon on the daylight side about 75 miles from the base. At this location, the Moon's day has just begun (daytime on the Moon lasts about 2 Earth weeks). Your spacecraft is in need of repair, and your survival depends on reaching the Moon base as soon as possible.

Of the 15 items that were not damaged in the crash, which would be most important for the trip? Rank the items from most important (#1) to least important (#15), then compare your rankings with those assigned by experts.

—— box of matches

—— food concentrate

—— 50 feet of nylon rope

—— parachute silk

—— solar-powered heating unit

—— two .45 caliber pistols

—— one case of powdered milk

—— two tanks of oxygen

—— stellar map of the Moon's constellations

—— self-inflating raft that uses carbon dioxide canisters for inflation

—— self-igniting signal flares

—— magnetic compass

—— 5 gallons of water

—— solar-powered FM walkie-talkie

—— first aid kit containing needles (for vitamins, medicine, etc.) that will fit through a special aperture in spacesuits

turn the page to see rankings by experts

EXPERTS' RANKINGS

1. two tanks of oxygen, essential for survival

2. 5 gallons of water, to replace the tremendous liquid loss on the lighted side of the Moon

3. stellar map of the Moon's constellations, your primary means of navigation

4. food concentrate, an efficient means of supplying energy requirements

5. solar-powered FM walkie-talkie, used for communication with the rescue party at the Moon base (Note: FM requires line-of-sight transmission and short ranges.)

6. 50 feet of nylon rope, for scaling cliffs

7. first aid kit: the vitamins, medicines, etc., help to sustain health

8. parachute silk, to provide protection from the Sun's rays

9. self-inflating life raft: the CO_2 bottle in it may be used for propulsion

10. signal flares, specially designed for an environment with no oxygen, for sending distress signals

11. two .45-caliber pistols, a possible means of self-propulsion when fired

12. one case of powdered milk, useful but bulkier than food concentrate

13. solar-powered heating unit: not needed unless you are on the dark side

14. magnetic compass: worthless for navigation because the magnetic field on the Moon is not polarized

15. box of matches: virtually worthless because there is no oxygen on the Moon to sustain flame

SKY HIGHS

Q **Is the Moon the only celestial body that has phases?**

A No. All of the planets have phases, but only Mercury and Venus, the two planets between the Sun and Earth, go through all four phases: new, first quarter, full, and last quarter. Mars, Jupiter, Saturn, Uranus, Neptune, and Pluto never have a new or quarter phase because more than half of their surface is always lit by the Sun as viewed from Earth.

FACTOID

The best time to view any planet that is farther from the Sun than Earth is when it is on the opposite side of the sky from the Sun, or in opposition. At that time, it is close to Earth and visible all night, if there is no cloud cover.

Q **If equinox means "equal night," why aren't there exactly 12 hours of daylight and 12 hours of night on the spring (vernal) and fall (autumnal) equinoxes?**

continued

We measure days and equinoxes differently. An equinox begins everywhere in the world when the center of the rising Sun touches the horizon, and it ends 12 hours later when the center of the setting Sun touches the horizon again. A day begins when the upper edge of the rising Sun touches the horizon (a few minutes before the center) and ends when the upper edge of the setting Sun touches the horizon (a few minutes after the center). On the equinoxes, daylight and darkness are not equal in duration because of those few minutes. (Remember: Don't look at the Sun without eye protection!)

FACTOID

On any given day, the Sun is visible when it is just below the horizon at sunrise and sunset. Earth's atmosphere refracts, or bends, light rays from the Sun so that they arc over the horizon. As a result, the Sun appears higher than it actually is.

Q Why are there no sounds in the vacuum of outer space?

A There is essentially nothing there. Vibrating matter (air or other material) pushes and pulls whatever is around it in pulses, causing sound waves. These waves of energy can travel only through matter, which does not exist in the vacuum of space. There are atoms and molecules floating about but not enough to make a difference.

FACTOID

Sound waves are not radio signals; those can travel in a vacuum. Astronomers use radio telescopes to study radio signals emitted by many objects in space, including the Sun.

Q Has the Moon always been the same distance from Earth?

A No. Some 4 billion years ago, the Moon was about 14,000 miles away, looming gigantically in the sky. It is slowly drifting away from Earth, currently at about 1.5 inches each year, because tidal forces are causing the lunar orbit to expand. Today, the Moon is about 238,855 miles from Earth. In a few billion years, the Moon will stop drifting. Then, one side of Earth will face the Moon all of the time, just as one side of the Moon always faces Earth.

FACTOID Due to the Moon's elliptical orbit, the distance between the Moon and Earth varies. The closest orbital point (perigee) has been as little as 221,451 miles; the farthest point (apogee) has been as much as 252,731 miles.

Q Is Earth perfectly round?

A No. Try this: Gently squeeze a round grape at top and bottom. That's Earth—flattest at the poles and fattest around the middle. The shape is due to Earth's rotation. If you stood at the North or South Pole, you'd be about 13 miles closer to Earth's core than if you stood at the equator.

FACTOID Because of Earth's shape, the point farthest from the center of Earth is the top of Ecuador's Mt. Chimborazo (altitude: 20,702 feet), which is near the equator.

OUR BEAUTIFUL BUT DEADLY SISTER

Venus has long been considered Earth's "sister" planet because the two have much in common. Recent discoveries reveal their differences.

Ancient Romans named Venus for the goddess of love and beauty, and it is the only planet named for a girl. You have probably seen Venus: After the Sun and Moon, it is the brightest object in the sky.

Because Venus makes dazzling appearances both before sunrise and after sunset, people thought that it was two separate stars. It is known as the morning star when it rises before the Sun in the east and as the evening star when it sets after the Sun in the west. Venus can not be seen in the middle of the night.

At its closest approach, 26 million miles, Venus is the planet closest to Earth, but it's no place like home.

The diameter of **Venus** is 7,522 miles; the average diameter of **Earth** is 7,926 miles.

The gravity on **each planet** is almost the same.

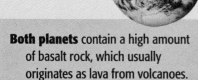

V E N U S

A comparison in size between Venus and Earth, to scale.

E A R T H

Venus, the second planet from the Sun, is located between Mercury and Earth.

Both planets contain a high amount of basalt rock, which usually originates as lava from volcanoes.

Venus reflects 65 percent of the sunlight that strikes it.

Earth reflects 37 percent of the sunlight that strikes it.

Venus's atmosphere is more than 96 percent carbon dioxide, with no oxygen.

Earth's atmosphere is about 0.036 percent carbon dioxide and about 21 percent oxygen.

Venus has no water.

Earth has salt and fresh water.

A year on **Venus** has 225 Earth days.

A year on **Earth** has 365 (sometimes 366) days.

CONTINUED

THE PRESS OF AIR PRESSURE

The air of our atmosphere presses on us all the time. Because we are used to living with the force of air pressure at or near sea level and because the air we breathe into our bodies balances the outside pressure, we don't feel the weight of air. However, at high elevations, air pressure decreases because there are fewer air molecules. Think of what happens if you climb or drive up a mountain or take off in an airplane: Your ears pop. This is your body's way of balancing the pressure inside and outside your ear.

The high air pressure on Venus would be like being about 3,280 feet underwater on Earth.

The air pressure (the force or weight of tiny air molecules) on **Venus** is about 90 times greater than that on **Earth.**

Venus has no moons.

Earth has one moon.

The weather on **Venus** seldom changes, with heavy sulfuric acid clouds, acid rain that evaporates before it reaches the surface, slow winds near the surface, and strong winds in the upper atmosphere.

The weather on **Earth** is variable, with clear to cloudy periods; clouds that produce rain, ice, or snow; and light to hurricane-force winds.

The mean temperature on the surface of **Venus** is about 900°F.
The mean temperature on the surface of **Earth** is about 60°F.

An artist's rendering of the surface of Venus

Venus rotates on its axis in 5,832 hours, or 243 Earth days, so its year (225 Earth days) is shorter than its day.

Earth rotates on its axis in 24 hours, or 1 day.

Venus rotates backward, or in retrograde. If you were on **Venus,** the Sun would rise in the west and set in the east.

Earth rotates forward. On **Earth,** the Sun rises in the east and sets in the west.

SAY WHAT? "VENUTIAN" refers to the planet Venus.

"VENETIAN" refers to Italy's city of canals, Venice.

⬆ In 1962, U.S. NASA spacecraft *Mariner 2* flew by Venus, becoming the first spacecraft to send back information about another planet.

⬆ From 1990 to 1994, *Magellan,* a U.S. NASA spacecraft, mapped 99 percent of Venus's surface with radar.

➡ In 2005, the *Venus Express* spacecraft was launched from Russia. It traveled for 153 days to Venus, where it used solar-powered instruments to study the planet's clouds and atmosphere.

CCCP

⬇ On May 20, 2010, the Japanese Aerospace Exploration Agency (JAXA) launched *Akatsuki,* designed to study Venus with four cameras and an ultraviolet imager. However, the spacecraft failed to enter Venus's orbit. *Akatsuki* will encounter Venus again in 2015. As of October 2012, JAXA was planning for *Akatsuki* to attempt to enter Venus's orbit in 2015 or 2016, depending on the spacecraft's condition.

⬆ During the 1960s, '70s, and '80s, the Soviet Union sent 16 spacecraft named *Venera* to Venus. As some of these parachuted into the atmosphere, they were crushed before they landed. *Venera 7,* in 1970, was the first to return data from the surface of another planet; it radioed back reports about Venus's atmosphere and temperature. Later *Venera* spacecraft survived long enough to send back photos, results from soil and air tests, and radar maps.

How to Tell Time by the STARS

Merak

Dubhe

The Big Dipper

North Star

Ever wonder how, before analog and digital clocks, people figured out what time it was after sunset? On clear nights, they looked at the stars. You can, too.

First, find the Big Dipper, part of Ursa Major. It looks like a pot with a long handle. (Do not confuse it with Ursa Minor, the Little Dipper, which looks like a small pot.)

Now find the stars opposite the Big Dipper's handle. Named Merak and Dubhe, these are called "pointer stars" because an imaginary line through them points toward the North Star, which is also known as Polaris. The imaginary line made by the pointer stars is the "hour hand" of your imaginary star clock.

Find the North Star.

In northern latitudes, the Big Dipper constantly revolves around the North Star and never sets, which is why it is called a circumpolar constellation. The Big Dipper makes one revolution around the North Star in 23 hours, 56 minutes, and 4 seconds—that's almost once per day, making it almost a 24-hour clock.

TO TELL TIME

Draw a circle on a piece of paper. This will be a 24-hour clock, and the hour hand will turn backward, or, counterclockwise. Put 24/0 at the top; this is midnight. Write 12, for

noon, at the bottom. Where 9 would normally be on a clock, write 6; this stands for 6:00 A.M. Write 18 where 3 would normally be on a clock; this stands for 6:00 P.M. Fill in the rest of the numbers accordingly.

At night, under clear skies, hold the clock in the air, with 24 at the top. Check the position of the Big Dipper and the North Star. Notice the direction of the imaginary line between them and draw the hour hand at that angle in the circle, with the North Star at the circle's center. On March 6, you can read the time right off the clock. If the hand is pointing to 23, this means 11:00 P.M. If the date is not March 6, you're not finished.

◆ **If the date is after March 6,** count the number of months after March 6 (include quarter fractions, if necessary), double it (×2), and subtract that number from the time.

EXAMPLE: On December 9, the Big Dipper clock reads 20 hours. December 9 is about 9 months after March 6. Nine doubled equals 18. So, 20 − 18 = 2:00 A.M.

EXAMPLE: On July 20, the Big Dipper clock reads 5 hours. July 20 is about 4.5 months after March 6. Double 4.5 to get 9. Thus 5 − 9 = −4 = 4 hours before midnight = 8:00 P.M. But wait!

➡ When calculating star time during Daylight Saving Time (between the second Sunday in March and the first Sunday in November), add 1 hour to the result. So the real answer is 9:00 P.M.

◆ **If the date is before March 6**—say, in January—you can do as above (January is 10 months after March 6) or use a slightly different formula. Count the number of months before March 6, double it, and add that number to the star time.

Remember that through the night, the imaginary hand will advance counterclockwise (backward) in a complete cycle over 24 hours. With practice, you will be able to tell time at night within 15 to 30 minutes.

⇨ **40 DEGREES NORTH**

This technique for telling time works best in areas north of 40 degrees north latitude, about half of the United States and all of Canada.

WET

ne of Mother Nature's most powerful events is a HURRICANE, also called a typhoon in the Western Pacific and a cyclone in the Indian Ocean. These massive, wet storms—the result of several thunderstorms that cluster together—develop near the equator, over ocean water that is at least 80°F.

Hurricane conditions occur when winds near the ocean's surface are blowing in the same direction and at the same speed. This causes warm, moist air to rise into the atmosphere. The stronger the winds blow, the more air rushes in to replace the rising air. As the air rises, it cools and changes to rain. The winds and rising air feed on each other, causing a storm that increases in size and strength. The rotation of Earth causes the storm system to rotate as it moves westward. This is called the Coriolis effect.

'n' WILD

warm, moist air rises, cools, and changes to rain

winds flow outward, allowing the air below to rise

ocean winds blow in the same direction

rain bands

eye

'ROUND AND 'ROUND IT GOES

• • •

North of the equator, hurricanes rotate counterclockwise.

South of the equator, hurricanes rotate clockwise.

continued ➡

The speed of the wind determines how a storm is categorized:

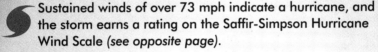 Wind speeds of up to 38 miles per hour indicate a tropical depression.

Sustained winds of 39 to 73 mph indicate a tropical storm; at this stage, it is given a name by the National Hurricane Center.

Sustained winds of over 73 mph indicate a hurricane, and the storm earns a rating on the Saffir-Simpson Hurricane Wind Scale (*see opposite page*).

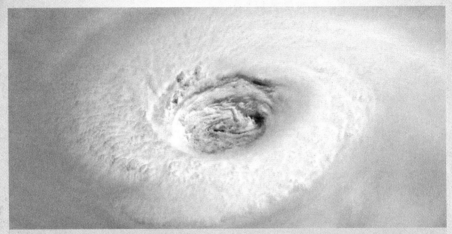

Astronauts on the International Space Station took this photo of Hurricane Igor forming in the Atlantic Ocean on September 14, 2010. At the time this photo was taken, winds were at a sustained 132 mph, or Category 4 on the Saffir-Simpson scale.

As the storm rotates, it forms an "eye" in its center. The eye can be from 5 to more than 100 miles across, depending on the speed of the rotating winds. On average, an eye is about 30 miles wide.

Weather conditions in the eye are usually calm and clear, with very little wind and rain. When the eye of a hurricane passes overhead, it may actually be sunny and nice! However, the most damaging winds, the thickest clouds, and the heaviest rainfall occur in the eyewall, the area immediately surrounding the eye.

Hurricanes need to be over warm water to maintain their strength. Soon after a hurricane makes landfall, its winds weaken. If a hurricane goes back out to sea, it can regain its strength; if it continues inland, its winds continue to weaken, but heavy rains may still occur.

How to Measure

Hurricane Strength

The Saffir-Simpson Hurricane Wind Scale assigns a rating from 1 to 5 based on a hurricane's intensity. It is used to give an estimate of the potential property damage from a hurricane landfall. Wind speed is the determining factor in the scale, as storm surge values are highly dependent on the slope of the continental shelf in the landfall region. Wind speeds are measured at a height of 33 feet (10 meters) using a 1-minute average.

CATEGORY 1 **Average wind: 74–95 mph.** Significant damage to mobile homes. Some damage to roofing and siding of well-built frame homes. Large tree branches snap and shallow-rooted trees may topple. Power outages may last a few to several days.

CATEGORY 2 **Average wind: 96–110 mph.** Mobile homes may be destroyed. Major roof and siding damage to frame homes. Many shallow-rooted trees snap or topple, blocking roads. Widespread power outages could last from several days to weeks. Potable water may be scarce.

CATEGORY 3 **Average wind: 111–129 mph.** Most mobile homes destroyed. Frame homes may sustain major roof damage. Many trees snap or topple, blocking numerous roads. Electricity and water may be unavailable for several days to weeks.

CATEGORY 4 **Average wind: 130–156 mph.** Mobile homes destroyed. Frame homes severely damaged or destroyed. Windborne debris may penetrate protected windows. Most trees snap or topple. Residential areas isolated by fallen trees and power poles. Most of the area uninhabitable for weeks to months.

CATEGORY 5 **Average wind: 157+ mph.** Most homes destroyed. Nearly all windows blown out of high-rises. Most of the area uninhabitable for weeks to months.

HURRICANE SEASON in the Atlantic basin (Gulf of Mexico, Caribbean Sea, and Atlantic Ocean) runs from June 1 to November 30.

TYPHOON SEASON in the Pacific Ocean runs from May 15 to November 30.

continued

A U.S. Air Force WC-130J Hurricane Hunter plane powers down after returning from its final flight into Hurricane Irene in August 2011.

FLY IN THE EYE

▶ The U.S. Air Force has a fleet of aircraft that fly into hurricanes. The planes drop special equipment to gather data such as wind speed, air pressure, humidity, and temperature, which help researchers to determine a hurricane's size. On July 27, 1943, Colonel Joseph Duckworth piloted the first plane that purposely flew into the center of a hurricane.

CALL IT BY ITS NAME

- The word "hurricane" is believed to be based on the Caribbean god Huracán, who could summon violent storms in the tropics.

- Later, hurricanes were identified by their longitude and latitude.

- Clement Wragge, a British meteorologist working in Australia in the late 1800s, first gave tropical storms classical, biblical, and personal names.

- In the 1940s, U.S. military meteorologists named storms after their girlfriends and wives.

- In 1953, the National Hurricane Center started naming storms.

DID YOU KNOW ?

The scientific term for a hurricane is **tropical cyclone.**

The fear of hurricanes (or tornadoes) is called **lilapsophobia.**

Hurricane, West Virginia, was named after nearby Hurricane Creek, which was named by a party of surveyors commissioned by General George Washington. The men noticed a group of trees that were bent in one direction, as if struck by a hurricane.

Hurricane, Utah, got its name from Hurricane Fault, which was named when a whirlwind blew the top off a buggy in which a group of surveyors was riding. (A hurricane has never struck this area and is not likely to because it is so far inland.)

■ ■ The first Atlantic Ocean storm named for a man was Hurricane Bob in 1979.

The second Hurricane Bob, 1991

■ ■ When a hurricane causes extreme destruction, its name is retired and not used again. Charley, Dean, Ike, Isabel, Katrina, Rita, Sandy, Tomas, and Wilma are among the names retired. The first man's name, Bob, was used again in 1991. The second time around, Bob was such a fierce storm that he was retired, too!

■ ■ Tropical storms are named alphabetically; each year, the names alternate between male and female. Atlantic names beginning with the letters

Q, U, X, Y, and **Z** are never used.

➡ **Are You a Storm?**
For a list of this year's hurricane names, go to **Almanac4kids.com/Calendar.**

■ ■ If all of the alphabetical names are used in one season, Greek letters are used. In 2005, six Greek-letter names were needed: Alpha, Beta, Gamma, Delta, Epsilon, and Zeta.

continued ➡

Members of the Methodist Episcopal Church South (now called Providence United Methodist Church) in Swan Quarter, North Carolina, wanted a plot of land on which to build a new church. When the land they wanted was not for sale, they chose a different plot and erected a church.

On September 16, 1876, a hurricane hit! The wind and high water moved the new church off its brick pilings. The church floated down the street and settled on the originally selected plot. A marker by the church reads "Moved by the Hand of God."

"Gulf rising, water covers streets of about half of city."

At 3:30 P.M. on September 8, 1900, this message was sent to Washington, D.C., by a weatherman in Galveston, Texas, which had been struck without warning by a hurricane. By 6:30 P.M., the water was up to a man's neck. With rain and high winds, the water continued rising for hours, eventually reaching 15 feet, wiping out almost the entire city, and causing more than 8,000 deaths. It was the worst natural disaster to ever strike the United States.

DOUBLE TROUBLE

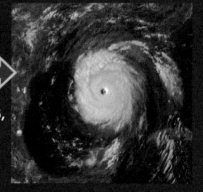

On August 29, 2005, Hurricane Katrina devastated the coastal regions of Louisiana, Mississippi, and Alabama. On September 24, 2005, Hurricane Rita made landfall on the Texas/Louisiana border. Both storms reached Category 5 status on the Saffir-Simpson Hurricane Wind Scale.

Animals may be smarter than we think.

WATCH, LISTEN, AND SEE WHAT THE WEATHER WILL BE!

When horses and mules are lively without apparent cause, expect **COLD.**

When dogs eat grass, it will be **RAINY.**

If a cat licks itself with its face turned toward the north, the **WIND** will soon blow from that direction.

When cows bellow (a deep, loud cry) in the evening, expect **SNOW** that night.

A goat will utter its peculiar cry before **RAIN.**

Before a **STORM,** sheep become frisky, leap, and butt (or box) each other.

Hogs rubbing the sides of their pens in winter indicates an approaching **THAW.**

When foxes and wolves bark and utter shrill cries, expect violent **WIND** and **RAIN** within 3 days.

When the field mouse makes its burrow with the opening to the south, expect a **SEVERE WINTER;** when to the north, expect much **RAIN.**

BE A WEATHER WATCHER

People have been recording and sharing their observations about weather for centuries as artwork, journals, sayings, and proverbs. Weather records help to track trends, such as cycles, from one season and one year to the next. They also help us to make many choices, including how to dress, when to plant and harvest or take a vacation, even where to live. Many years of records may help to indicate changes in our climate.

Gather as much information as you can every day at the same time of day; if possible, note the date and time. Include conditions such as

YOU WILL NEED:
notebook or pad of paper
pen or pencil
thermometer
clock
computer

- **temperature**
- **precipitation (fog, snow, rain)**
- **wind speed and direction**
- **cloud type and amount of cover**

CLICK QUICK

FOR LOCAL DETAILS

Go to
Almanac4kids.com/Weather
for conditions in your area:

Click on "change location,"
then key in your zip code.

Click on "GO" under
"Know Your Clouds!"
for pictures, names, and
descriptions of clouds
that may appear over
your head.

As you become better at recording weather conditions, use the **international weather symbols** to abbreviate your weather data. This code was developed in the early 1800s, and is used by pilots, sailors, meteorologists, and weather hobbyists. Professional weather cartographers (mapmakers) became so skilled in using these symbols that they could quickly record a location's weather in a space that could be covered by a dime!

CATCH THE WIND

Reproduce this compass (or a portion of it) in your notebook to show the wind direction for each day. Make sure that the arrow points away from where the wind is coming from. (Use the sunrise and sunset locations to help you determine the compass points in your area.)

SOME INTERNATIONAL WEATHER SYMBOLS

Weather Conditions

•	light drizzle
••	steady, moderate drizzle
•••	steady, heavy drizzle
•	light rain
••	steady, moderate rain
•••	steady, heavy rain
✳	light snow
✳✳	steady, moderate snow
✳✳✳	steady, heavy snow
△	hail
∽	freezing rain
⊗	sleet
)(	tornado
�	dust devil
⤙	dust storm
≡	fog
⊓	thunderstorm
‹	lightning
⸮	hurricane

Sky Coverage

○	no clouds
◔	two- to three-tenths covered
◔	four-tenths covered
◑	half covered
◕	six-tenths covered
◕	seven- to eight-tenths covered
●	completely overcast

HIGH CLOUDS

⌣	cirrus
౨	cirrocumulus
2	cirrostratus

MIDDLE CLOUDS

◡	altocumulus
∠	altostratus

LOW CLOUDS

—	stratus
⌓	stratocumulus
//	nimbostratus

VERTICALLY DEVELOPED CLOUDS

⌓	cumulus
⊠	cumulonimbus

continued

Use the BEAUFORT WIND FORCE SCALE below to help to determine wind speed.

The Beaufort Wind Force Scale is a common way of estimating wind speed. It was developed in 1805 by Admiral Sir Francis Beaufort of the British navy to measure wind at sea. We can also use it to measure wind on land.

Admiral Beaufort arranged the numbers 0 to 12 to indicate the strength of the wind from calm, force 0, to hurricane, force 12. Here's a scale adapted to land.

"Used Mostly at Sea but of Help to All Who Are Interested in the Weather"

Beaufort Force	Description	When You See or Feel This Effect	Wind Speed (mph)	Wind Speed (km/h)
0	Calm	Smoke goes straight up	less than 1	less than 2
1	Light air	Wind direction is shown by smoke drift but not by wind vane	1–3	2–5
2	Light breeze	Wind is felt on the face; leaves rustle; wind vanes move	4–7	6–11
3	Gentle breeze	Leaves and small twigs move steadily; wind extends small flags straight out	8–12	12–19
4	Moderate breeze	Wind raises dust and loose paper; small branches move	13–18	20–29
5	Fresh breeze	Small trees sway; waves form on lakes	19–24	30–39
6	Strong breeze	Large branches move; wires whistle; umbrellas are difficult to use	25–31	40–50
7	Moderate gale	Whole trees are in motion; walking against the wind is difficult	32–38	51–61
8	Fresh gale	Twigs break from trees; walking against the wind is very difficult	39–46	62–74
9	Strong gale	Buildings suffer minimal damage; roof shingles are removed	47–54	75–87
10	Whole gale	Trees are uprooted	55–63	88–101
11	Violent storm	Widespread damage	64–72	102–116
12	Hurricane	Widespread destruction	73+	117+

SERVICE

In the United States, the importance of weather reporting became official with the establishment of the Weather Bureau in 1870. Its employees collected weather observations from military posts and other places across the country. They used the telegraph to issue warnings about approaching storms to citizens in communities in the East. (In the United States, winds tend to blow from west to east, meaning that weather often moves in that direction.)

1894

William Eddy, using five kites to lift a self-recording thermometer, makes first observations of temperatures aloft.

The government begins using balloons and airplanes to conduct upper-air atmospheric research.

1904

A hurricane warning service is established.

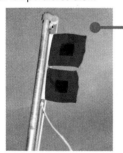

1935

1960

The world's first weather satellite, *TIROS I,* is launched from Cape Canaveral, Florida, on April 1.

1970

The Weather Bureau is renamed the National Weather Service.

1975

The National Weather Service installs new supercomputers with the ability to make 69.7 trillion weather calculations per second (up from 14 trillion in 2007).

The first "hurricane hunter" satellite is launched into orbit.

2009

continued

RECORD

George Washington

- For generations, Native Americans on the Great Plains recorded weather events in pictorial calendars called *waniyetu wówapi* (winter count), beginning and ending with the first autumn snowfall.

- A study of weather records in farmers' journals and diaries as well as newspapers dating from the 1700s indicates that early frosts in New England destroyed crops and left many people hungry.

- Beginning in January 1785, George Washington recorded the temperature daily, usually in the morning, at noon, and at sunset, sometimes indoors and sometimes outdoors. (In those days, the temperature of a room that faced north and did not have a fire in the fireplace could have been similar to the temperature outdoors.)

The oldest continuous WEATHER RECORD in North America

is maintained at the Blue Hill Meteorological Observatory, which sits on top of Great Blue Hill in Milton, Massachusetts, at an elevation of 635 feet. The stone observatory was begun by 24-year-old Abbott Lawrence Rotch. He built it with his brother and opened it with fireworks on January 31, 1885.

Thomas Jefferson

- In 1804 and '05, explorers Meriwether Lewis and William Clark noted temperature, wind direction, and general conditions, sometimes twice a day.

- Thomas Jefferson kept weather records. He noted that on July 4, 1776, the day on which he signed the Declaration of Independence, it was 76°F in Philadelphia, Pennsylvania.

- By regulation, lighthouse keepers maintained records of weather and daily events.

➡ **Abbott began keeping a weather diary in 1881.**

➡ **The oldest mercury barometer still in daily use is at the observatory.**

➡ **The coldest temperature ever observed at Blue Hill, –21°F, was recorded on February 9, 1934.**

➡ **The highest temperature ever observed at Blue Hill, 101°F, was recorded on August 10, 1949. It was matched on August 2, 1975.**

➡ **Ski slopes were built on Blue Hill in the 1930s, and skiers, especially kids, still hit the slopes every winter.**

Abbott Lawrence Rotch

Weird, Huh?

Why do these things never happen when we're around to see them?

If you've experienced weird "weather" or similar events, tell other kids at

Almanac4kids.com /TellUs

Spider Riders

The Great Cobweb Storm occurred in October 1881, on the shores of Lake Michigan, from Sheboygan to Milwaukee, Wisconsin. The sky was thick with white webs, from minuscule pieces to 60-foot-long strands. It is believed that this event was caused by certain species of migratory spiders that cast their silk on a breeze and ride the wind to a new location.

BUGNADO BLITZ

In June and July 2011, at around sunset, some folks in Iowa living near the Missouri River noticed "smoky" clouds around treetops, above ditches, and near cornfields. Instead of fog or haze, it was a swirling swarm of bugs! Record flooding that

APPLE CRISP

In the late afternoon of December 12, 2011, more than 100 small apples rained from the sky, striking car windshields and denting automobile hoods along a 60-foot stretch of road in Keresley, Coventry, England. Officials from the British Weather Service concluded that volatile conditions present at the time may have spawned an updraft that blew the fruit off trees or lifted it off the ground and into the upper atmosphere, until turbulent air calmed and the apples fell to Earth.

FISH FLY

On three different occasions—in 1974, 2004, and 2010—hundreds of 2-inch-long whitefish have fallen from rain clouds onto Lajamanu, in Australia's Northern Territory. Officials at the Australian Bureau of Meteorology believe that the fish were transported up by a thunderstorm and carried to altitudes of 40,000 feet or more, before showering down on the small town, which is 326 miles from the nearest river!

year resulted in an above-normal bug population. The "bugnadoes" occurred for about 2 weeks. Then, it seems, birds and dragonflies had them for lunch.

LIFE

AT ONE END OF THE

ANTARCTICA is the size of the United States and Mexico combined. No town exists on this vast continent, but there are several research stations. Of those, only one is at the southernmost point on Earth—Amundsen-Scott South Pole Station. About 150 scientists, technicians, cooks, and others live and work there during the summer. Just before winter arrives, 100 of them head north to warmer places.

When "Polies" (the name for people who live there) look out through the windows of this station, they see ice, ice, and more

Ski-equipped Hercules LC-130 aircraft flew all of the station's components, plus the equipment required to assemble them, to the South Pole. The Hercules engine never shuts down, as the cold would make it nearly impossible to restart it.

ice. Ice covers more than 97 percent of Antarctica (the ice contains about 90 percent of all of the fresh water on Earth). The station sits on a flat slab of ice that is 9,000 feet thick and 9,306 feet above sea level. It is like being on a mountain without a peak. The ice drifts about 33 feet every year.

Despite all of the ice, Antarctica is considered a

The elevated Amundsen-Scott South Pole Station was built atop the 9,000-foot-thick polar ice sheet.

ANTARCTICA

Geographic South Pole

O → Amundsen-Scott South Pole Station

Southern

Ocean

South Magnetic Pole

WORLD

desert because the humidity in the air is low and the continent gets only 7 to 9 inches of snow each year. (Because the wind blows almost constantly, snowfall is hard to measure.) The snow usually falls as small, sparkling ice crystals called "diamond dust"; snowflakes are rare. Because the temperature is so low, the snow never melts!

Frigid darkness prevails at the South Pole for about 6 months, with sunlight reappearing on the equinox in September and increasing until the solstice in December. Then, daylight begins to diminish and is gone on the equinox in March, when the cycle begins again.

SOUTH POLE STATION STATS

HIGHEST RECORDED TEMPERATURE

9.9°F

LOWEST RECORDED TEMPERATURE

-117°F

ANNUAL AVERAGE TEMPERATURE

-57°F

DECEMBER MONTHLY AVERAGE*

-18°F

JULY MONTHLY AVERAGE*

-76°F

AVERAGE WIND SPEED

12.3 mph

PEAK WIND GUST RECORDED

55 mph, in August 1989

*Summer in the Southern Hemisphere occurs from December through March; winter, from June through September.

continued

A SHORT HISTORY
of SOUTH POLE HOUSEKEEPING

The first explorers known to have reached the South Pole were led by Norwegian Roald Amundsen. He and four others arrived on December 14, 1911. (Whale and seal hunters may have gone before.) The temperature was –7.6°F. The explorers set up camp and spent 3 days checking calculations to confirm that they had truly reached the pole. Before departing, they took pictures and planted a flag, leaving behind the tent, extra equipment, and a note. About a month later, on January 17, 1912, British explorer Robert Scott arrived with four men. The temperature had dropped to –22°F. In addition to being weary, cold, and malnourished, Scott and his team were disappointed not to be the first to the pole. They died during their return journey to base camp.

In 1956, as part of Operation Deep Freeze, the United States began building a station at the South Pole, and researchers have been there ever since. As interest in learning more about the Antarctic grew, the station grew. A dome was erected in the 1970s.

After the first station and then the dome were buried by drifting snow, engineers and architects designed the current station with 36 stiltlike columns that can lift the entire building up to 24 feet higher. Now, winds and drifting snow blow over and under it. As the ice shifts under the station, the columns are adjusted to keep it level.

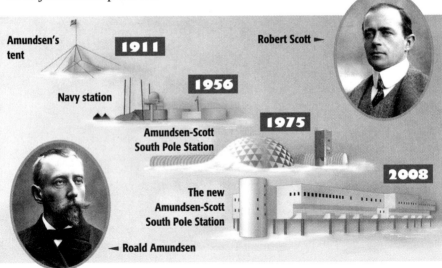

Amundsen's tent

1911

Robert Scott

Navy station

1956

Amundsen-Scott South Pole Station

1975

The new Amundsen-Scott South Pole Station

2008

Roald Amundsen

The new building, which opened in January 2008, is bigger than a football field, and life in it is close to normal:

▶ Polies must wear 25 pounds of clothing to stay warm; they store the clothes in a special coat room.

▶ Bedrooms (two sizes: 9x8 feet for winter residents and 9x7 feet for summer visitors) have just enough space for a bed and a desk.

▶ In winter, kitchen supplies must last 265 days to serve 50 very hungry people. On average, a Polie must eat 5,000 calories a day to have enough energy to keep warm; most actually lose weight!

▶ Salad greens and vegetables are grown in a greenhouse and served fresh at meals.

▶ Polies relax and warm up in the sauna.

▶ All trash and waste are packed in recycling rooms to be shipped out. (Everything travels by ship or aircraft, but not in winter.)

▶ For entertainment, Polies have rooms for reading, games, and arts and crafts. They also have a TV room, where they watch recorded programs (the South Pole is too remote to receive live TV), and a small store for buying snacks.

▶ Polies lift weights or play basketball in the gym.

▶ A doctor and medical equipment are available. Serious injuries require creative thinking: In 2002, a meteorologist fell and hurt his knee. Using voice and video links, doctors in Boston helped a doctor at the South Pole perform surgery on the man.

▶ Beneath the station, in carved-out areas in the ice, are fuel and cargo storage, waste management, maintenance garages, and a power plant. A cylindrical tower contains stairs and an elevator so that people can travel back and forth from the aboveground building to the underground facilities.

A cutaway view of the new Amundsen-Scott South Pole Station. This diagram was prepared by the National Science Foundation to illustrate some of the features of the station.

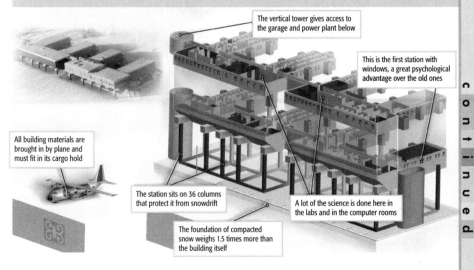

The vertical tower gives access to the garage and power plant below

This is the first station with windows, a great psychological advantage over the old ones

All building materials are brought in by plane and must fit in its cargo hold

The station sits on 36 columns that protect it from snowdrift

A lot of the science is done here in the labs and in the computer rooms

The foundation of compacted snow weighs 1.5 times more than the building itself

continued

POLE POSITIONS

The **geographic South Pole** is the southernmost place on Earth, the spot where Earth spins on its axis. An official stake and sign mark the spot, which is just outside South Pole Station. They are moved every New Year's Day because they sit atop sheets of moving ice.

Not far away sits a **ceremonial South Pole,** which has red and white stripes and is often where photos are taken. It is surrounded by the flags of the 12 countries that signed the Antarctic Treaty in 1959, setting aside Antarctica as a scientific preserve.

Both the ceremonial pole and the official stake are occasionally moved to keep them within walking distance of the geographic South Pole.

The **magnetic South Pole,** 1,800 miles from the geographic South Pole in the Southern Ocean, is where compass needles point in the Southern Hemisphere. This spot also moves because Earth's magnetic field is always changing.

The **pole of inaccessibility** is the spot on any continent that is the farthest inland, away from any ocean. In 1958, the Soviets built a small research station on this spot in Antarctica, but it was later abandoned.

Flags fly at the ceremonial South Pole to signify the 12 original nations of the Antarctic Treaty: Argentina, Australia, Chile, Russia, New Zealand, Norway, USA, UK, France, Japan, Belgium, and South Africa.

COLDEST JOURNEY ON EARTH

▶ On March 21, 2013, a team organized by Sir Ranulph Fiennes began an attempt to become the first people to cross Antarctica in winter. The team planned to travel about 2,000 miles on skis, with their equipment, including living quarters and a laboratory, on sledges dragged behind them by bulldozers. Temperatures were expected to be as low as −130°F—a risk for the men and the machines—during the 6-month expedition.

EXTREME SCIENCE

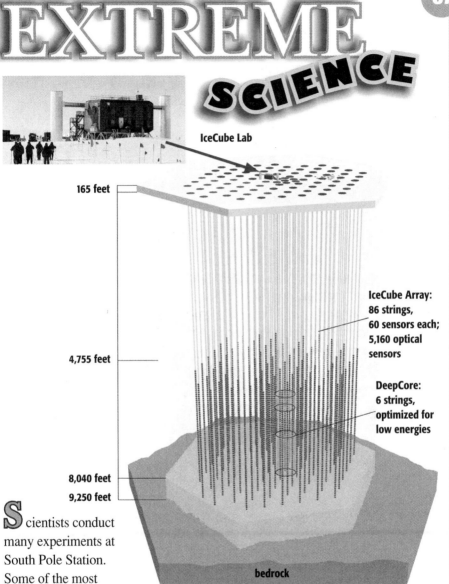

IceCube Lab

165 feet

IceCube Array: 86 strings, 60 sensors each; 5,160 optical sensors

4,755 feet

DeepCore: 6 strings, optimized for low energies

8,040 feet

9,250 feet

bedrock

S cientists conduct many experiments at South Pole Station. Some of the most unusual involve a unique telescope. Called IceCube, this tool is made up of thousands of digital optical modules and is buried 1½ miles deep in the ice (it's longer than the height of the world's three tallest skyscrapers combined), where it searches for subatomic particles called neutrinos. When neutrinos interact with ice, a blue light is produced and the IceCube telescope studies them.

SWAMP THINGS!

Swamps can be creepy . . . until you get to know them.

Think of a swamp as a giant sponge. It's an area of low-lying land that soaks up nearby water and is covered with trees or bushes. Swamp water can be deep or shallow, fresh or salty.

People used to think that swamps were useless and sometimes drained them. Many valuable swamplands have been lost to agriculture and development, so it's important to preserve those that remain.

Scientists now realize that swamps provide food and habitat for many types of plants and animals. Some animals, such as American crocodiles, depend on them to survive. Swamps also help to rid water of certain pollutants and to control flooding.

Major League SWAMPS

G rab your hip boots! Swamplands exist all over the world, waiting to be explored. Here are a few:

1 Atchafalaya Swamp, Louisiana, is the largest swamp in the United States. Atchafalaya is a Native American word that means "long river."

2 The Everglades, Florida, nicknamed the "River of Grass" after a book by that title, is a vast area in southern Florida. Everglades National Park covers over 2,500 square miles.

3 The Great Dismal Swamp is in Virginia and North Carolina and is protected as a National Wildlife Refuge.

4 The Pantanal, in Brazil, is one of the largest wetlands in the world.

5 The Sudd is a huge area in Sudan, Africa, that borders the Nile River. During the rainy season, this swamp can grow to be as big as England.

6 The Vasyugan, another of the largest swamps in the world, sits on the border between Siberia and Central Asia.

continued ⇨

Who Eats WHOM?

The Swamp Food Chain

The food cycle starts with plants and small life forms such as insect larvae; next come fish, frogs, lizards, and snakes; then come birds and larger mammals.

Who Goes There?

A Dozen Swamp Creatures from A to Z

For many species of wildlife, swamps are a welcoming habitat teeming with water, food, shelter, and superb nesting spots.

Here's a look at a few types of swamp-dwellers, as well as a few surprising swamp "visitors"—animals that stop in to hunt, reproduce, and nest, later moving to a different habitat.

Anacondas have been called "masters of the swamp" for good reason. These South American water snakes can grow to nearly 30 feet long and weigh 1,200 pounds. Other snakes may be longer, but anacondas are the heaviest in the world. They conquer by twisting their body into what some call the "evil loop," squeezing their prey into submission and then swallowing these animals live, head first. (You can relax: Anacondas rarely attack humans and eat only once or twice a year.)

Armadillos are lazy, sleeping up to 16 hours a day in burrows near swamps. Their armorlike shells make them easy to identify as they lumber around in the morning and evening hunting for beetles, ants, and other bugs. They have poor vision but a great sense of smell, and long, sticky tongues that can lick ants right out of the ground—up to 40,000 ants in one meal!

green anaconda

nine-banded armadillo

continued ➡

Shy, secretive **bobcats** don't like to be seen, but they are fierce, strong hunters who kill larger animals by suddenly pouncing on them. About twice the size of a house cat, these meat-eaters also snack on smaller animals like mice and birds. Their name comes from their tail, which looks as though it has been cut off, or "bobbed." Bobcats live in a wide variety of habitats, including swamps.

Beware of the many sharp teeth of the **caiman,** which can be found lurking in the swamps of Central and South America. Like alligators and crocodiles, it's classified as a "crocodilian." Various species of caimans range in length from 5 to 16 feet long. Caimans eat a variety of foods, including, sometimes, other caimans.

What's the largest rodent in the world? That would be the **capybara,** found in South American swamps. These big "rats" look like giant guinea pigs; live in groups; can grow to be 4 feet long and about 1½ feet high; and weigh more than 100 pounds. Good divers and swimmers, they can remain underwater for as long as 5 minutes. They live in groups and are fun to watch.

Despite being endangered or extinct in many areas of North America, **cougars** still stalk Florida's swamplands, where they're called panthers. (They're also called pumas, mountain lions, and catamounts.) These large cats can weigh as much as 225 pounds and be 7 or 8 feet long. Cougars make many sounds, including a loud scream known as a "caterwaul."

During the dinosaur age, **dragonflies** with 27-inch wingspans once flew through the air. Several species of giant dragonflies still fly in Australian swamps, although their wingspans are about 5 inches. These modern giants are beautiful but poor flyers.

bobcat

caiman

capybara

cougar

dragonfly

flamingo

manatee

Flamingos are easy to spot, and their distinctive pink color comes from the food they eat, such as algae or insects. They live in groups on lakes and swamps, where they nest in mounds of mud. Sometimes they move together so well that they look like a marching band. In East Africa, more than a million flamingos have been known to gather, forming the largest flocks of birds in the world.

Manatees are huge beasts that can weigh more than 1,000 pounds. Also known as "sea cows," they stay on the move, slowly swimming to warmer waters during cold weather. These plant-eaters are gentle, with few natural enemies, but they are sometimes hit and killed by speedboats.

Many birds can be found in swamps, including **swamp sparrows,** which have long legs for wading. These birds often stick their heads underwater in hope of catching a swimming snack.

Water striders are made for swamps, with their special ability to walk (and even run) on water. Their secret is hairy legs: Microscopic hairs trap tiny air bubbles that keep these bugs afloat.

Many different species of **zooplankton** live in various swamps. Zooplankton are tiny, floating invertebrates that often live near the water's surface, where they play an important role in the food chain, providing tasty treats for fish and many other swamp creatures.

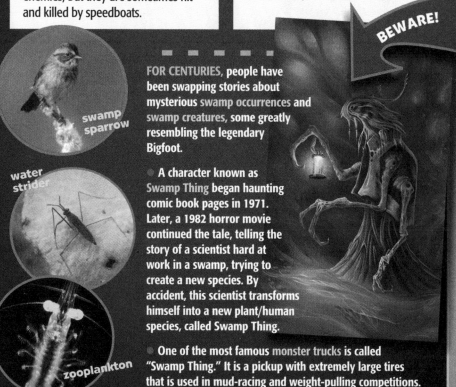

BEWARE!

swamp sparrow

water strider

zooplankton

FOR CENTURIES, people have been swapping stories about mysterious swamp occurrences **and** swamp creatures, **some greatly resembling the legendary Bigfoot.**

● **A character known as** Swamp Thing **began haunting comic book pages in 1971. Later, a 1982 horror movie continued the tale, telling the story of a scientist hard at work in a swamp, trying to create a new species. By accident, this scientist transforms himself into a new plant/human species, called Swamp Thing.**

● **One of the most famous** monster trucks **is called "Swamp Thing." It is a pickup with extremely large tires that is used in mud-racing and weight-pulling competitions.**

OCEAN

Our Earth has only one oceanic

PACIFIC OCEAN

ATLANTIC OCEAN

The **Atlantic Ocean** is named after the Greek mythological figure Atlas, who was said to be strong and to carry the world on his back.

The **Pacific Ocean** (the largest) was named by Portuguese explorer Ferdinand Magellan in 1520. He was leading a fleet of ships from Spain, in search of a western route to the Spice Islands. In late November, his three remaining ships sailed into what Magellan described as a "beautiful, peaceful ocean." Its name became Pacific, from the Latin word for peaceful.

The **Southern Ocean,** once called the Antarctic Ocean, surrounds the continent of Antarctica and was renamed in 1999. This ocean's large, strong, circumpolar current carries 150 times more water than all of the world's rivers combined. When it flows near the strong currents in the Atlantic, Pacific, and Indian oceans, it mixes with their waters. The Southern Ocean's fierce

water, but different parts of it have different names.

ARCTIC OCEAN

The **Arctic Ocean** (the smallest) is named for the region around the North Pole. The word "arctic" comes from the ancient Greek *arktos,* or bear, for the bear constellations Ursa Major and Ursa Minor, which include Polaris, the North Star.

The **Indian Ocean** is named for the subcontinent of India, the name of which in turn comes from the Indus River. Early Persian explorers could not properly say the "s" in *sindhu,* the Sanskrit word for "river." Their pronunciation of *"hindu"* later became *"indos"* and *"indus"* to invading Greeks and Romans, respectively.

INDIAN OCEAN

In Greek mythology, Poseidon became ruler of the sea.

winds and storms, sea ice, and icebergs have made its waters the least explored in the world. Its currents, sea ice, and cold waters can affect climate everywhere.

CONTINUED

SOUTHERN OCEAN

DID YOU KNOW?

- The word "ocean" comes from the Greek word *Okeanos*.

- 19th-century Russian oceanographer Yuly Shokalsky came up with the words "world ocean" to describe all of the water.

- Ocean water covers more than 70 percent of Earth's surface.

In 1768, when **Benjamin Franklin** was joint postmaster general of the American colonies, he noticed something strange: It took two weeks longer for ships carrying mail to sail from England to the colonies than for ships to sail from the colonies back to England. Why? he wondered.

Franklin spoke with a sea captain, who told him about a current in the Atlantic Ocean that he called the "gulf stream." The gulf stream caused ships going to England, in the direction of its flow, to speed up and caused vessels traveling to the colonies, or against the stream, to slow down. Soon after that, Franklin made the first map of the Gulf Stream *(shown below)* and helped to make it well known.

Now we know that the Gulf Stream influences the weather on the east coast of North America and the west coast of Europe.

Drowned Out?

In Greek mythology, Oceanus ruled the ocean, which was believed to be a great river that circled Earth. He married Tethys, and the couple had 3,000 daughters and 3,000 sons, all called Oceanids—the spirits of rivers, waters, and springs. Oceanus and Tethys were eventually overthrown, and Poseidon and his wife, Amphitrite, became rulers of the sea.

In 1979, in waters off the island of Oahu, Hawaii, a submersible carried oceanographer and undersea explorer **SYLVIA EARLE** 1,250 feet below the ocean's surface—deeper than any living human being had ever reached. She then explored the seabed, walking untethered for 2½ hours in a pressurized suit. Today, she is sometimes called "Her Deepness," and *Time* magazine designated her its first "hero for the planet" for her decades of scientific research. Earle believes that the ocean has no borders and that we must all work together to protect it.

Our Earth is about 70 percent water and 30 percent land. What if these percentages were reversed? Here is one artist's map of what this very different world might look like:

Once found throughout northern North America, the gray, or timber, wolf is now most commonly found in Canada; Alaska; and some northern states, particularly Minnesota, Wisconsin, and Michigan. The gray wolf population was about 2 million in 1600. Today, it is about 75,000.

Wolves are intelligent and social and live in packs of 4 to 15, led by an adult male. They make dens in caves, hollow logs, or burrows. A female usually gives birth to four to seven pups in the spring. (Most are born with blue or gray eyes that later turn to yellow or brown.)

F U N F A C T

The Japanese word for wolf means "great God."

aoooo

*Q What did the wolf say when someone stepped on its foot?

The pups stay with the parents for up to 2 years. Other wolves in the pack help to care for the pups when the parents are out getting food.

When hunting, wolves work together in the pack to kill moose, caribou, elk, and deer, often smelling them from more than a mile away and seeing them in the dark. A wolf's sense of smell is more than 100 times greater

than that of a human, and a light-reflecting layer on its eyes helps with night vision. They also capture and eat hares and rabbits, beavers, small rodents, birds, and insects. A hungry wolf can eat 20 pounds of meat in a single meal! Berries are a favorite snack.

Owwwww!*

WHY WOLVES HOWL

- to signal the pack to meet up
- to signal its location to the rest of the pack
- to warn other wolves to stay away from the pack's territory
- group howling produces harmonies that trick listeners into thinking that there are many more wolves present than is actually the case

WHEN WOLVES HOWL (or not)

- when hunting, especially during the evening and early dawn
- in winter, when they seek out mates
- not at the Moon: Experts have found no connection between the phases of the Moon and wolf howling.

 Aooooowwwww!

CONTINUED ▶

HOW WOLVES HOWL

They point their noses toward the sky because projecting the howl upward allows the sound to carry farther—up to 6 miles in the forest and 10 miles across treeless tundra.

FUN FACT

Some Native American tribes call the January full Moon the full Wolf Moon because it appeared when wolves howled in hunger outside the villages.

GRAY, EXCEPT WHEN IT ISN'T

The gray wolf's coat is typically light gray sprinkled with brown and black but may be pure white in the Arctic. In winter, its long, bushy tail, which is the same colors as its coat, helps to keep its face warm when it's sleeping.

FUN FACT

An adult gray wolf has 42 teeth, 10 more than an adult human.

Catch Him If You Can

➡ A wolf's two front paws, with five toes, are larger than its back paws, which have four toes.

➡ When walking, wolves usually place a hind paw in the track made by a front paw, making the tracks appear to be in a straight line. (Dog tracks tend to zigzag.)

➡ Wolves run on their toes, which stretches out their legs and gives them a long stride so that they can cover ground quickly.

➡ A wolf can sprint (run a short distance) as fast as 40 mph. It can run great distances at speeds of 15 to 30 mph.

➡ A wolf pack may travel from 30 to 125 miles in a day.

➡ Wolves can swim up to 8 miles at a time.

FUN FACT

🔫 Wolves were the first animals to be placed on the United States' Endangered Species Act list in 1973.

Can You Name the Big Bad Wolf?

The **Three Little Pigs** cartoon, released by Walt Disney in 1933, was based on a fairy tale about three pigs who each build a house—one of straw, one of sticks, and one of bricks—to protect themselves from the Big Bad Wolf. Do you know the wolf's real name?

Answer:
Zeke Midas Wolf

NO FOOLING!

 shepherd boy was watching his flock near the village and became bored. He thought that it would be fun to pretend that a wolf was attacking the sheep, so he cried out, "Wolf! Wolf!" The villagers came running to help him save the sheep from harm. The boy laughed when they discovered that there was no wolf.

He played the trick again, and then again. Each time, the villagers came to his aid, only to be fooled.

One day a wolf really did attack the sheep! The boy cried out "Wolf! Wolf!"—but this time, no one answered his call. The villagers thought he was playing games again. *–from Aesop's Fables*

The moral of the story:

☞ People who tell lies are not believed even when they speak the truth.

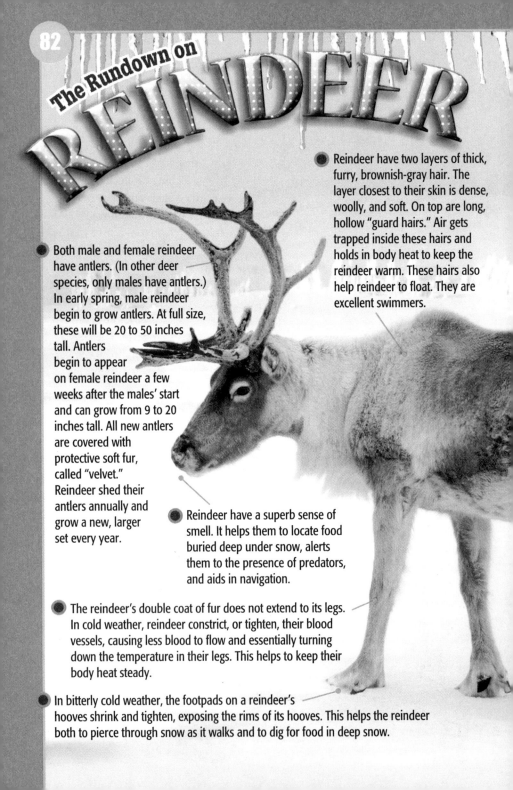

The Rundown on REINDEER

Reindeer have two layers of thick, furry, brownish-gray hair. The layer closest to their skin is dense, woolly, and soft. On top are long, hollow "guard hairs." Air gets trapped inside these hairs and holds in body heat to keep the reindeer warm. These hairs also help reindeer to float. They are excellent swimmers.

Both male and female reindeer have antlers. (In other deer species, only males have antlers.) In early spring, male reindeer begin to grow antlers. At full size, these will be 20 to 50 inches tall. Antlers begin to appear on female reindeer a few weeks after the males' start and can grow from 9 to 20 inches tall. All new antlers are covered with protective soft fur, called "velvet." Reindeer shed their antlers annually and grow a new, larger set every year.

Reindeer have a superb sense of smell. It helps them to locate food buried deep under snow, alerts them to the presence of predators, and aids in navigation.

The reindeer's double coat of fur does not extend to its legs. In cold weather, reindeer constrict, or tighten, their blood vessels, causing less blood to flow and essentially turning down the temperature in their legs. This helps to keep their body heat steady.

In bitterly cold weather, the footpads on a reindeer's hooves shrink and tighten, exposing the rims of its hooves. This helps the reindeer both to pierce through snow as it walks and to dig for food in deep snow.

- ➡ **A female reindeer is a** cow.
- ➡ **A male reindeer is a** bull.
- ➡ **A baby reindeer is a** calf.
- ➡ **A group of reindeer is a** herd.
- ➡ **Reindeer and caribou are** cousins.

What Do You Know About Reindeer?

Reindeer love cold places. (You probably won't see any reindeer roaming around your neighborhood unless you live near the Arctic.) Everything about reindeer, from their sense of smell to the shape of their hooves, helps them to survive and be comfortable in snow and frigid temperatures.

LAPPS LOVE THEM

Lapland is an area covering parts of northern Scandinavia and Russia. Centuries ago, Lapps, or Sami people, the nomadic inhabitants of Lapland, relied on reindeer for basic needs.

● **In winter, both men and women wore coats and breeches,** or pants, sewn from reindeer skins, which were also used, when filled with dry grass, to make shoes (no socks needed!) and mittens. For extra warmth, they slept on reindeer skins.

● **Lapps consumed reindeer milk, cheese, and meat** (tongue and marrow were delicacies). The meat was often preserved by drying or smoking.

● **Reindeer aided in transportation, pulling carriages and sleds,** sometimes at up to 20 miles per hour. Adding reindeer fur to the bottom of skis prevented skiers from sliding backward.

● **Today, many Lapps still herd reindeer** and keep the ancient traditions alive.

continued

Can you name Santa's eight reindeer?
(Answer below.)

Q What do reindeer play in their stalls?

• • •

A Stable tennis.

GAMES
That Reindeer (and People) Play

➡ **Why are reindeer hitched to Santa's sleigh?**

Reindeer are the only species of deer that can be domesticated. For more than 2,000 years, they have been used to carry and pull loads.

● In winter in Oulu, Finland, everyone goes to the Reindeer Carnival. Events include reindeer lassoing, sled racing, and sprint racing, with snacks of reindeer soup and other reindeer delicacies.

● In Finnish Lapland, at the annual festival of St. Mary, reindeer race while pulling a skier behind them.

● At the Fur Rendezvous (or Rondy) in Anchorage, Alaska, a couple of dozen reindeer run along a designated street in the Running of the Reindeer. People dress in costumes and run among the reindeer, trying to reach the end of the course ahead of them.

Answer: Dasher, Dancer, Prancer, Vixen, Comet, Cupid, Donner, Blitzen. The poem that made these reindeer famous was written by Clement Clarke Moore in 1822. Dunder and Blixem were the original names from Moore's poem, but they have changed over time to Donner and Blitzen. Rudolph the Red-Nosed Reindeer appeared much later, in 1939.

ROACH-O-RAMA!

Cockroaches have been on Earth for about 350 million years. (That's about 348 million years longer than people!) The earliest of those years, the Carboniferous period, is sometimes known as the Age of Cockroaches because they were everywhere.

Today, most of the world's 4,000 types of cockroaches live in tropical forests, where they feed on the lush vegetation. About 60 of the 4,000 species live in North America. Four of the most common are . . .

The **BROWN-BANDED COCKROACH,** named for two brown bands across its abdomen. It prefers temperatures above 80°F and lives in the dry, secluded parts of a house—on bookshelves, inside electric clocks, and in closets and stationery drawers. It grows to be about half an inch long and especially enjoys eating wallpaper paste and glue from the backs of envelope flaps.

The **GERMAN COCKROACH,** also known as the Croton bug, steam fly, or steam bug. This half-inch-long insect likes to spend the winter in restaurants, hotels, and nursing homes in northeastern states. Unable to survive in areas away from human activity, it eats chocolate bars, ice cream, cake, and bread crumbs (even if they are in the garbage!) because they contain sugar and carbohydrates.

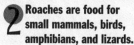

Why We Like Them (even a little)

1 Roaches are omnivores (they eat anything) and thereby help to clean up our environment.

2 Roaches are food for small mammals, birds, amphibians, and lizards.

continued

The **ORIENTAL COCKROACH**, also known as a waterbug. This insect seeks out damp, shady areas such as basements and crawl spaces. It grows to be about an inch long, eating garbage and sewage.

The **AMERICAN COCKROACH**, which thrives in hot weather. It is usually found in the basement drainage system of homes and in sewers. In cooler weather, it seeks out heating ducts and steam tunnels. The diet of this 2-inch-long critter includes paper, hair, decaying bread, fruit, fish, and fermenting foods.

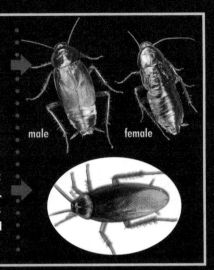

male   female

Why We Don't Like Them

1 Studies have shown that 98 percent of cockroaches carry at least three types of bacteria that may cause food poisoning.

2 Cockroaches can spread diseases such as typhoid fever, dysentery, cholera, and tuberculosis.

Yum or Yecch?

Individual cockroach species have different favorite foods, but most will eat just about anything organic. They especially like . . .

- human poop and cockroach droppings
- pet food
- bananas
- boiled potatoes

- sweet foods, such as cinnamon rolls
- empty egg cartons
- dead or disabled members of their own species

➡ Cockroaches do NOT like cucumbers, which upset their stomachs.

Christopher Columbus called cockroaches *cucaracha,* from the Spanish word for caterpillar, *cuca.*

• • •

Many cockroach species can fly.

• • •

A cockroach can live for up to a month without its head.

• • •

Cockroaches can detect movements of less than a millionth of a millimeter in the surface they inhabit.

• • •

Young cockroaches can squeeze into a space as thin as a dime (1.35 millimeters), while adults can get into a space no bigger than a quarter's thickness (1.75 millimeters).

• • •

Cockroaches can not run for long, but they are fast. The American cockroach has been clocked at a speed of 50 body lengths per second (which is like a human sprinting at 210 miles per hour!).

• • •

Cockroaches are nocturnal: They work at night and, often, in the dark. If you turn the lights on, they will run away.

• • •

DON'T TURN YOUR HOME INTO A
ROACH MOTEL

For centuries, humans have tried to stop, banish, or kill **COCKROACHES**, with little success. These insects are quick, crafty, and adaptable. You can take precautions against them, however:

➡ Put away food when you are done with it and clean up crumbs.

➡ Store food in glass, plastic, or metal containers with lids.

➡ Do not leave dirty dishes lying around.

➡ Throw away old stamps and envelopes.

➡ Inspect boxes before bringing them into the house.

➡ Block off cracks in walls and cabinets.

➡ Fix any leaking pipes.

➡ Never bring cockroaches into your house!

Turn a Patch — Into a Storybook

Mr. McGregor's Cabbage

When Mrs. Rabbit went shopping, she warned her children—Flopsy, Mopsy, Cottontail, and Peter—not to go into Mr. McGregor's garden. Everyone but Peter obeyed her and hopped down the lane to pick blackberries. Peter went straight to Mr. McGregor's garden to nibble on beans, lettuce, and other vegetables. When Mr. McGregor spotted Peter, he chased him. Scampering away, Peter lost one shoe in the cabbages and another in the potatoes, and then he caught the button of his jacket on a fence. Just as Mr. McGregor was about to catch him, Peter wriggled out of his jacket. He ran all the way home, where his mother scolded him for losing his clothes. Peter went to bed, while Flopsy, Mopsy, and Cottontail enjoyed their berries.

—adapted from The Tale of Peter Rabbit
by Beatrix Potter

Grow Your Own

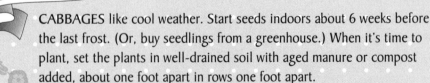

CABBAGES like cool weather. Start seeds indoors about 6 weeks before the last frost. (Or, buy seedlings from a greenhouse.) When it's time to plant, set the plants in well-drained soil with aged manure or compost added, about one foot apart in rows one foot apart.

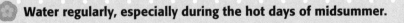

Water regularly, especially during the hot days of midsummer.

children's tales centuries ago.

Garden

continued

Watch for cabbageworms and remove them whenever you see them.

Pick cabbage heads when they are full but before they crack or split. After harvesting the main head, smaller heads may grow on the remaining stem. Pick these when they are firm and about 3 inches in diameter.

Did You Know?

The world's largest cabbage weighed 125.9 pounds and measured 21 inches in diameter.

The word coleslaw comes from the Dutch word *koolsla*. *Kool* means "cabbage" and *sla* means "salad."

Q Why do cabbages win races?

A *Because they know how to get a-head!*

When he was playing baseball on hot summer days, baseball legend Babe Ruth kept cool with a cabbage leaf. He placed several leaves on ice in a cooler. When the leaves were cold, he trimmed them so that they fit under his cap. One medium-size cabbage leaf kept the top of his head cool for three innings.

☞ Prepare for a Hefty Harvest

Even a storybook garden needs real-life conditions. Choose a sunny area for your garden. Remove any weeds and rocks and mix a couple of inches of compost or aged manure into the dirt. If you grow in a pot, make sure that the pot has drainage holes in the bottom. Mix aged manure or compost into the potting soil.

Cinderella's Pumpkin

A long time ago, a handsome prince needed a wife. To find one, he held a great ball, to which he invited all of the young ladies in his kingdom. Cinderella's stepmother would not let her go. On the evening of the dance, Cinderella was at home alone, when suddenly her fairy godmother appeared! She cast a spell, turning a pumpkin into a golden carriage and Cinderella's rags into a beautiful outfit, including a pair of glass slippers. She told Cinderella to go to the ball, but that she must return home by midnight or her dress would turn into rags and the carriage back into a pumpkin.

At the ball, Cinderella was dancing with the prince when the clock struck midnight. As she ran from the ballroom, she lost a glass slipper.

The next day, the prince went looking for the young lady whose foot would fit into the slipper. When Cinderella tried on the slipper, it fit perfectly, and she and the prince lived happily ever after.

–adapted from the Cinderella folktale

Grow Your Own

You can grow a PUMPKIN that, when mature, looks like the one that became Cinderella's coach. Officially, it's called 'Rouge Vif D'Etampes', also known as Cinderella's pumpkin. Like other varieties (including one called 'Fairytale'), it likes 75 to 100 days (or more) of warm weather and needs lots of room (50 to 100 square feet) to grow. When all danger of frost has passed, make two or three small hills of well-drained soil, with aged manure or compost added, about 5 to 6 feet apart.

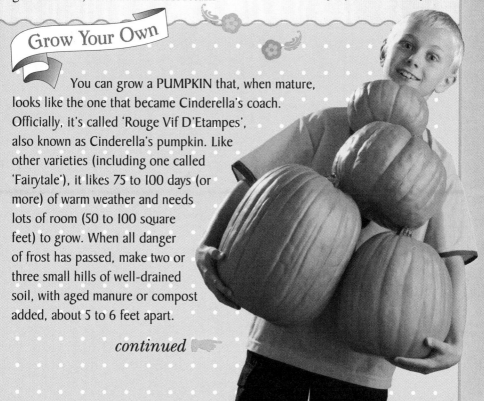

continued

Plant four or five seeds one inch deep in each hill. When the young plants are about 2 inches tall, remove the weakest ones, leaving the strongest two or three plants.

Weed around your pumpkin plants regularly. Weeds compete with the pumpkin for nutrients and water.

Water about 1 inch per week, especially in early summer and during long dry periods.

Did You Know?

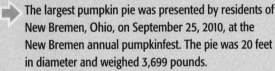

The world's largest pumpkin was grown by Ron Wallace from Greene, Rhode Island. It weighed 2,009 pounds.

The largest pumpkin pie was presented by residents of New Bremen, Ohio, on September 25, 2010, at the New Bremen annual pumpkinfest. The pie was 20 feet in diameter and weighed 3,699 pounds.

Pumpkin regatta races are held in Nova Scotia, Maine, Oregon, and Vermont every year. Contestants carve out gigantic 1,000-pound pumpkins and race them as boats.

 How do you fix a cracked pumpkin?

 With a pumpkin patch.

Jack's Bean Stalk

On the way to the market to sell his family's cow, Jack met a man who offered to trade him some magic beans for the cow. Jack happily did the trade. When he returned home with beans instead of money, his mother became angry and threw the beans out the window.

By the next morning, the beans had grown into a giant bean stalk. Jack climbed the stalk up into the sky, where he discovered a road. He followed it to the home of a giant and went inside. When he heard the giant returning home, Jack hid. He kept quiet and listened to the giant counting money. When the giant wasn't looking, Jack stole a bag of the giant's coins and climbed down the bean stalk.

Jack went up the bean stalk two more times to steal the giant's riches. On the third trip, the giant chased Jack down the bean stalk. When Jack was safely on the ground, his mother cut down the bean stalk, killing the giant, and Jack and his mother lived happily ever after.

—adapted from the Jack and the Beanstalk folktale

Grow Your Own

Plant GREEN BEANS in well-drained soil with aged manure or compost added when all danger of frost has passed. Choose from two types: Pole beans form vines and need stakes or poles to support them as they climb. Bush beans grow one foot high and do not need supports.

Plant pole bean seeds 4 to 6 inches apart in rows about 30 inches apart or in hills (four to six seeds per hill) 30 inches apart. For fairy tale–like long vines, choose the 'Jack in the Beanstalk' heirloom variety or scarlet runner beans. Plant bush bean seeds 2 to 4 inches apart in rows 18 to 24 inches apart.

continued

Be careful not to disturb beans' shallow roots when weeding.

Pick green beans before the seeds inside start to bulge and when the plants are dry, not wet. Wet picking may spread bacteria.

Did You Know?

Yardlong beans are similar to climbing green beans, but each pod can grow as long as 30 inches.

Green beans are also called snap beans because when you break them into pieces, they make a snap sound. They are also called string beans because some varieties have a long string that runs the length of the "seam" of the pod.

"Green" beans also can be white, red, yellow, or purple.

Q What do you call a retired vegetable?

A A has-bean.

Tell a New Tale

- Design a seed packet for cabbage, pumpkin, or beans. Include characters from the story and growing advice.

- Choose a different vegetable (or fruit) and write a story about it.

THE SALSA Princesses

How three
kids who
love food
contests
on TV
conducted
a salsa
tasting . . .

To Hannah, gardening was what old ladies did when there was nothing good on TV. At 11 years old, she loved to watch TV, especially on the big screen in the cool comfort of the air-conditioner when the Texas summer sun roasted the air outside. She hemmed and hawed when her grandmother asked her to help with planting tomatoes, peppers, and onions.

"Oh, okay," Hannah sighed. She put on her plastic high heels, picked up her purse, and followed her grandmother out the door.

continued➡

The girls gardened each morning for several

Katie, Hannah's sister, and Charli, their cousin, both 8-year-olds, were already in the garden.

"Ew-w-w!" Katie screamed gleefully each time she uncovered a worm.

"I want to do it!" cried Charli, when their grandmother dug a hole for a tender plant or filled the watering can.

Hannah watched and then stepped carefully into the freshly tilled soil, her heels almost disappearing into it. "What can I do, Grandma?" she asked. She laid her purse on the grass and reached for a trowel. Before long, the girls were singing Taylor Swift songs as they scooped soil, watered the seedlings, and labeled the rows.

The girls gardened each morning for several days. Grandma showed them how to hammer a wooden stake into the end of each row and stretch a string between the stakes, and Hannah forgot about TV, even her favorite cooking shows. The girls learned to dig a trench beneath the string with the edge of a hoe. Then they pushed nearly 100 tiny 'Texas Sweet' onion plants, some as thin as straws, into the bottom of the trench. They also planted four jalapeño pepper plants and a row of cilantro seeds. When they finished, the garden contained the ingredients for their favorite summer food, salsa, and all three girls had to redo their bright blue nail polish.

Several weeks of watering and weeding followed. One day, the girls practiced cheerleading in the garden to encourage the plants to grow. As the tomatoes swelled and took on a crimson blush, anticipation for the first taste of garden-fresh salsa ran high. One evening, Katie said, "Let's have a contest to see who can make the best salsa."

The other two girls snatched up Katie's idea like a fumbled football.

"Ew-w-w!" Katie screamed gleefully each time she uncovered a worm.

days . . . and Hannah forgot about TV. . .

"We'll need judges," said Charli.

"And rules," said Hannah. "And we'll mix our recipes in private so that no one else knows what goes into them."

They dropped the hose and raced to the house, tossing ideas back and forth as they went.

While they waited for a few more tomatoes to ripen, Hannah consulted a Mexican cookbook,

Charli, Katie, and Hannah select tomatoes for their salsa recipes.

and all three checked the pantry for ingredients. With Grandma, they made a trip to the spice aisle in the grocery store to purchase the items they didn't have in stock, including extra tortilla chips.

When enough tomatoes finally ripened, the girls gathered them in buckets, along with the onions and jalapeños. They dug out the aprons that they'd bought at the church auction and decided on the rules. They agreed on a blind taste test, with each batch of salsa identified only by a numbered sticker on its container, and they decided that the judges could not talk about the entries among themselves.

On the appointed day, the ingredients stood in a scarlet pyramid on the kitchen table. Each contestant selected a few tomatoes, an onion, and a couple of peppers. Lindsay, Hannah's aunt, took out her camera.

This commotion alerted the rest of the family—dads, moms, Grandpa, and three brothers and cousins—all of whom had volunteered as judges. They crowded into the kitchen as Grandma seeded the fiery jalapeños.

The food processor whirred as each girl prepared her secret salsa sensation. Once they had the basics chopped to their satisfaction, they banished the judges to the living room. From the cabinets and refrigerator shelves came the "extras"—canned tomato sauce, black pepper, cayenne pepper, garlic salt, chipotle powder, lime juice, and a bottle of chopped garlic. **continued➡**

No one spoke as they tasted again and again.

Hannah went out to the garden to cut fresh cilantro. They tasted, added ingredients, and tasted again.

After 20 minutes, the judges were called back into the kitchen. Each fixed a glass of ice water to clean their mouths between tastes. Grandma took the bowls of salsa into another room, where she numbered each bowl.

Charli grinds cilantro.

Each judge got a ballot, a pencil, and a paper plate heaped with chips. No one spoke as they tasted, sipped water, and tasted again and again. It was as exciting as a food competition on TV. When the judges were finished, Grandma left the room to count the votes.

Lindsay announced the winners and awarded princess banners as if it were a national beauty pageant:

"The second runner-up, who put in enough garlic to scare off vampires, is Katie."

"The first runner-up is Charli."

A scream went up as Lindsay said, "And this year's Salsa Princess, whose salsa is spicy enough to make steam shoot from your ears, is Hannah!"

Hannah accepted her banner graciously. "Wait," she said, and then she dashed to her room. She returned wearing a tiara and glittery lip gloss, ready for the camera. The Salsa Princess Competition was a spicy success!

Katie, Hannah, and Charli carefully mix their ingredients.

The winners! Katie, second runner-up; Charli, first runner-up; and Hannah, the Salsa Princess.

HANNAH'S WINNING

Salsa Recipe

1 medium onion

2 jalapeños, seeded

1 small bunch of cilantro, coarse stems removed

5 large ripe tomatoes, cored

1 can (8 ounces) plain tomato sauce

1 teaspoon freshly ground black pepper

2 tablespoons prepared chopped garlic in olive oil

1 teaspoon salt

1 tablespoon lime juice

½ teaspoon chipotle powder

¼ teaspoon cayenne pepper

Process the onion, jalapeños, and cilantro in a food processor until finely chopped and then pour into a bowl. Process the fresh tomatoes and add them to the bowl. Stir in the remaining ingredients. Serve with tortilla chips.

Makes about 3 cups.

SECRETS to growing GREAT TOMATOES and PEPPERS:

Plant tomatoes and peppers when the soil is warm. They love heat!

Put the plants in a place where they will get 6 to 8 hours of sun daily.

Plant them 2 to 3 feet apart.

Water daily for 2 weeks, then water deeply twice a week, depending on the weather.

PARTY with the

Any day—especially a warm, sunny one— is a good time to be outdoors. Set tables and chairs near the flowers, beside the vegetable patch, or on the lawn; gather friends; and have a garden party.

PLANTS

Choose an event or theme or mix a few:

- birthday
- last day of school
- first day of summer

- new friend
- going back to school
- vegetables and/or fruit

- flowers
- bugs and/or critters
- birds and/or butterflies

Invite Your Friends

Decorate construction paper or note cards with scraps of wrapping paper, stickers, clippings from magazines, or drawings. Include images of your theme, as well as your address, the date, and the time. Add your phone number or email address and tell guests to let you know if they are coming to the party.

Make Food for FUN

Prepare snacks that match the party theme. Turn the page for some suggestions.

➡ ➡ ➡

Spider Crackers

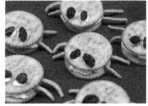

Spread cream cheese between two round crackers.

Ladybug Cupcakes

Frost your favorite cupcakes with red icing. With black frosting, make a large circle for a head at one edge of the cupcake. Add two dabs of white frosting and two mini chocolate chips for eyes. Place black jelly beans on the red frosting for spots. Add black string licorice for legs. Dye 1 cup of shredded coconut with green food coloring. Scatter it on the plate around the cupcakes for grass.

Insert chow mein noodles for legs into the filling. Add two dabs of cream cheese and two raisins for eyes.

Worm Juice

Several hours before the party, freeze gummy worms in ice cubes. Combine 1 part cranberry juice to 2 parts orange juice. Add 1 cup of sparkling water for fizz. You can also make lemonade or your favorite punch. Thoroughly wash a new watering can and use it as a pitcher. Serve the juice over the worm ice cubes.

Sunflower Sandwiches

Press a flower-shape cookie cutter into bread slices. Spread half with a favorite filling: peanut butter and jelly, hummus and cucumber, or cream cheese and raisins. Top with the remaining bread halves.

Veggie Patch Pizza

Pick (or purchase) basil, mushrooms, oregano, peppers, tomatoes, zucchini, onions, and other toppings. Ask an adult to help prepare and cook the pizza.

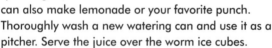

Edible Art

Set out vegetables (cherry tomatoes, sliced peppers, zucchini and radish slices), herbs (chives, parsley), dried fruit (cranberries, raisins), and snacks (chips, pretzels). Give each guest a small bowl of vegetable dip and ask them to create a face in it with the food.

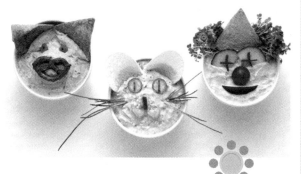

Artsy ACTIVITIES

Paint Rocks

YOU WILL NEED:

- a variety of stones
- acrylic paints
- brushes
- water
- clear varnish spray (optional)

Clean the stones and paint. If desired, spray with varnish when the paint is dry. Use as paperweights, doorstops, stepping-stones, or garden art.

Decorate Birdhouses

YOU WILL NEED:

- birdhouses (from a craft shop)
- acrylic paints
- brushes
- water
- buttons, beads, ribbon (optional)
- white glue (optional)
- wire

Spread newspaper on the work surface. Paint the house. When the paint is dry, glue on accessories, if desired. Attach a wire and hang from a tree or post.

continued ➡

Make Bird Feed Wreaths

YOU WILL NEED:

- grapevine wreaths
- florist's wire
- dried whole small sunflowers, other dried flowers and grasses, small pinecones, popcorn cobs
- ribbon

Using florist's wire, attach the bird food items to the wreath (largest items first). Add ribbon as decoration. Attach a wire loop to the back of the wreath and hang from a tree or post.

Grow a Garden in a Bottle

YOU WILL NEED:

- clean, 2-liter plastic bottle, cap on
- sharp knife
- scissors (optional)
- duct tape
- about 2 feet of string
- pebbles
- potting soil
- lettuce seeds or flower seedlings, such as pansies

cut a panel from the side of the bottle

punch a hole on each side of the cutout for string

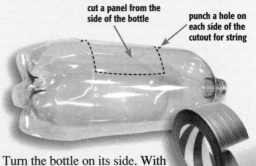

Turn the bottle on its side. With an adult's help, insert the knife about 2 inches from the bottom of the bottle and slice about halfway around the bottle, but no more than halfway. Insert the knife about 2 inches from the shoulder of the bottle and make a matching slice. Stand the bottle upright. Using scissors or the knife, cut out the panel of the bottle between the two slices. Fold duct tape over the edge of the cut. Make two holes for the string on the cut side of the bottle, one near the shoulder and one near the bottom. Insert one end of the string in each hole (the ends should be inside the bottle). Tie a knot on each end of the string so that it does not come out. Lay the bottle down, cut side up, and line the bottom with pebbles. Add potting soil to fill almost to the cut. Plant the seeds or seedlings. Water lightly. Hang the planter in sunlight. Water when the soil becomes dry.

Send Flowery Notes

YOU WILL NEED:

- construction paper
- scissors
- clear contact paper
- dried flowers

Fold the construction paper in half. Cut the contact paper to match the folded paper. Place the flowers on the "front" of the card. Peel off the contact paper backing and carefully cover the flowers with the sticky side. (It's okay if the flower petals move and get stuck under the contact paper.) Write a note to someone special.

Become a Bug

Make a hat or headdress inspired by a real or imaginary insect.

YOU WILL NEED:

- visors
- pipe cleaners
- pompom balls
- construction paper
- fabric scraps
- feathers
- beads
- ribbon
- scissors
- markers
- white glue
- stapler

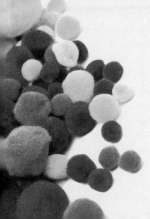

Using the items (and anything else you can think of), create wacky headgear. Make up a name for your species. Vote on the Most Scary, Most Creative, and Closest to Nature.

continued ➡

Make a Milk Jug Scarecrow

Make a garden character with a funny face, colorful clothes, and personal accessories.

YOU WILL NEED:

- metal clothes hanger
- round stick (broom or mop handle)
- duct tape
- plastic milk jug, washed and dried
- permanent markers
- white glue
- ribbon, straw, beads, glitter, necktie, hat
- old shirt
- twigs or gloves for hands

For shoulders, attach the clothes hanger about 4 inches from the top of the stick with duct tape. For the head, push the neck of the milk jug onto the stick as far as the tape. Use tape to hold the jug in place. Push the stick into the ground so that it will stand upright. (You do not need to do this in the garden. The goal is to steady the stick so that you can make the face and dress the character.) Draw a face on the jug. Use glue to add hair and other accessories to give your scarecrow personality. Hang the shirt on the hanger. Push twigs or gloves into the shirtsleeves for hands. Then give your scarecrow a name.

Fold Tissue Paper Flowers

YOU WILL NEED:

- colored tissue paper
- green pipe cleaners

Cut the tissue paper into same-size rectangles (try 8½x11 inches). Stack 10 to 15 pieces of tissue paper on top of each other. Working from the long side, fold the paper like an accordion. Wrap a pipe cleaner around the center of the pleated tissue paper. If desired, cut a pattern into the ends of the tissue paper. These will be the petals. Hold the flower at the center and separate each petal, pulling gently. Once all of the pieces are pulled, shape your flower to your liking.

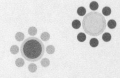

Hooray for Hummingbirds!

Invite these tiny birds into your yard.

Hummingbirds are all-American birds. They exist only in South, Central, and North America—nowhere else in the world. Altogether, there are 339 species of hummingbirds. In the spring, 21 species fly thousands of miles northward from Mexico, Costa Rica, and other southern places to visit the United States and Canada. In the fall, they return to their southern homes.

☐ A hummingbird has a tongue that is twice as long as its body.

Although hummingbirds usually weigh less than an ounce, these tiny birds have a lot of energy. When the wind blows in the direction that they are flying, they can travel up to 50 mph.

a female ruby-throated hummingbird

In North America, the greatest number and variety of hummingbirds can be found in western areas of the United States and as far north as Alaska. Only one species—the ruby-throated hummingbird—usually visits areas east of the Mississippi. The birds also visit southern Canada, especially British Columbia, Alberta, and Nova Scotia.

The best way to invite hummingbirds into your yard is to give them the basics:
☐ nectar
☐ water
☐ shelter to rest and maybe to nest

continued

Hummer Food

Hummingbirds' favorite food is nectar. This can be sugar water that you make or the sweetness of live flowers. Because these birds hover while they eat, flapping their wings at 80 beats per second, they prefer flowers that stand clear of other plants. The birds can feed more easily from some flower shapes than others:

deep, tubular flowers such as columbine or honeysuckle, into which the hummingbird can dip its beak

daisylike flowers such as Mexican sunflowers and zinnias because the yellow "button" in the middle is actually dozens of tiny nectar drinks

flower spikes such as gayfeather, penstemons, and salvias

Just as important as the shape of the flower is its color. Hummingbirds are strongly attracted to red, orange, pink, and blue.

Nectar for a Feeder

YOU WILL NEED:

2 cups water
½ cup granulated white sugar

Put the water into a pan and bring it to a boil on the stove. (Ask an adult for help.) Turn off the heat and add the sugar. Stir until the sugar dissolves. Cool the sugar water, then fill your bird feeder.

➡ *(Do not use honey in your feeder. It can give a hummingbird a tongue fungus.)*

Make a Feeder

Recycle a clean plastic soda bottle. Check a bird supply store or search the Web for "soda bottle feeder" and purchase a screw-on base feeder and hanger made specifically for attaching to the soda bottle.

➡ *If you buy a regular feeder, avoid one with yellow color.* Wasps are attracted to yellow.

Prepare a Place to Perch

The long flights and wing beating can make a hummingbird weary. As often as every 15 minutes, they look for a place to rest on trees and shrubs with small leaves. Particular plants include birch trees, butterfly bushes, and honey locusts. Don't worry if you do not have these plants in your yard— your hummingbird might also rest on your feeder's hanger.

Give a Bird a Bath

Set your garden hose to make a fine spray of water in one direction. Prop it to aim into the air. Watch—and listen—for hummingbirds dancing and singing in the shower.

Host Hummingbirds in a Garden

If you do not have the space to make a garden at home, talk to your teacher about planting these flowers at school or join with a friend or neighbor who would also enjoy having hummingbirds around.

Start small, with a few plants and a feeder. Add a plant or two each year. The plants will get bigger each year, and, before long, the hummingbirds will find them.

In addition to the flowers and plants mentioned, try these perennials:

Flowers
Bee balm
Cardinal flower
Coral bells
Dahlias
Daylilies
Delphiniums
Foxgloves
Hollyhocks
Hostas

Lupine
Maltese cross
Phlox
Speedwells

Vines
Cypress vine
Honeysuckle
Trumpet vine

Duck Tales

More than 150 different species of ducks exist in our world, and they are found in the wild on every continent except Antarctica.

Each year, U.S. farmers raise about 22 million ducks. Most of these are Pekin ducks, descendants of wild mallard ducks domesticated in Peking (now Beijing), China, several thousand years ago. Farmers like Pekin ducks because they tend to be calm, can't fly, and produce large eggs.

Ducks' natural habitat is marshland. Farmers must create this environment by providing a pond, if there is not water on their property. They also must provide fencing and shelter for their ducks to protect them from predators. When they are well cared for, ducks can live on a farm for as long as 10 years.

A duck's webbed feet have very little soft tissue and a unique blood-flow system that keeps the feet from freezing. Ducks can swim all year-round, even in winter's icy water. Webbed feet help ducks not only to paddle in water, but also to walk on mud and in wetlands.

Duck Designations

- A **drake** is a male duck.
- A **hen** is a female duck.
- A **duckling** is a baby duck.
- A **raft, team,** or **paddling** is a group of ducks in the water.
- A **brace** or **badling** is a group of ducks on the ground.
- A **brood** is a group of ducklings.
- A **flock** is a group of ducks in flight.
- A **sord** is a group of mallards in flight.

Dabbling for Dinner

The name "duck" comes from the Anglo-Saxon word *duce,* which means "diver." In fact, not all ducks dive for their food. Mallards are part of a group called "dabbling ducks." They feed on small insects and plants by tipping into shallow water, with their tails sticking up. Most barnyard ducks, including Pekins, are "dabblers," but mainly they just eat what the farmer feeds them—usually a mixture of corn, barley, and oats.

QUACKY FACTS

- **Not all ducks quack!** Hens quack. Drakes seldom do. They grunt, growl, and whistle. However, because ducks are social animals, if one is raised on a farm without the company of other ducks, it will begin to mimic the animals around it—cows, dogs, even chickens!

continued

Water Proof

Have you ever seen water roll off a duck's back? This is because its feathers have been waterproofed. The uropygial gland, near a duck's tail, produces oil, which the duck spreads over its outer feathers with its bill. Water doesn't mix with oil. On a duck, water forms a bead and rolls off. This oil helps the duck to float (wet feathers would weigh it down!) and keeps its fluffy inner feathers dry, which helps it to stay warm.

QUACKY FACTS

- **A duck's eye positions** allow it to have full, panoramic, 360-degree vision, without turning its head. Because of its range of vision and the fact that no more than half of its brain ever "sleeps" at the same time, a duck is usually able to detect a predator in less than a second.

Eggs-ellent

Duck eggs are good for you! They have a higher yolk-to-white ratio and are larger than chicken eggs, so they can furnish 24 percent more energy. Duck eggs provide higher amounts of protein, vitamins, and minerals than chicken eggs, as well as 50 percent more monounsaturated (helpful) fat. However, duck eggs also contain 19 percent more saturated (harmful) fat and twice as much (harmful) cholesterol, so they should be eaten in moderation as part of an overall healthy diet.

Natural light is a signal for hens to

DUCKS OVERBOARD!

chicken egg

duck egg

During a storm on January 10, 1992, almost 29,000 floating toys, including 7,000 "rubber" duckies, were lost overboard from a container ship in the middle of the Pacific Ocean. About 19,000 of the toys were captured by currents that took them south, with some going west—to Hawaii, Australia, and Indonesia—and others floating east, to end up on the western shore of South America.

The remaining 10,000 headed north, where they started showing up on the Alaskan coast 10 months later. This group eventually continued to the Arctic, where it got frozen into the pack ice, carried eastward across the Arctic Ocean, and released from thawed ice into North Atlantic waters, to begin showing up in New England (in 2000) before looping back across to the British Isles (in 2007).

Scientists have tracked the movement of these floating fleets to learn about ocean currents.

produce, which determines the mating and laying cycle in the wild. On the farm, egg production can slow in the winter months, when there isn't a lot of natural daylight. Because of this, many farmers use electric light bulbs to encourage egg laying.

Did You Know

Most "rubber" duckies are made from vinyl plastic, not rubber.

continued

Q Why does the farmer use a duck as an alarm clock? ➡ **A** It wakes him up at the quack of dawn.

Fowl Weather Signs

🔴 **Expect rain if ducks flap their wings repeatedly.**

🔴 When ducks quack profusely, they are said to be "calling for rain."

QUACKY FACTS

- **The Big Duck**

🔴 A dream of ducks swimming on clear water portends a lucky journey.

Once the site of widespread duck farming, Long Island, New York, is home to The Big Duck. In 1931, duck farmer Martin Mauer commissioned the construction of this duck-shape building 30 feet long and 20 feet tall to attract shoppers to his farm store in the town of Riverhead. The Big Duck has been moved (carefully!) several times. Now a gift shop, it stands 4 miles down the road in Flanders, where it is a National Historic Site.

ACTIVITIES

➡ **RACE THE DUCKS**

"Rubber" ducky races can be a fun way to raise funds for your school or community. Research this event, then write a proposal for making it happen. Consider where, when, and how to do it, as

Duck Sayings

Match these duck sayings with their meanings:

1 Like water off a duck's back

2 A sitting duck

3 Getting your ducks in a row

4 A lame duck

5 To duck out

6 Like a duck out of water

7 Just ducky

____ **A** A helpless or defenseless target or victim

____ **B** To escape doing something

____ **C** Being in an unfamiliar or uncomfortable situation

____ **D** Describing something that does not "get to you" (annoy or upset you)

____ **E** Fine, excellent, wonderful

____ **F** To get organized

____ **G** A politician whose effectiveness is reduced because his term of office is almost up

ON THE FARM

Answers: 1. D; 2. A; 3. F; 4. G; 5. B; 6. C; 7. E

well as what equipment you would need and how to publicize it. Ask a couple of teachers and parents to help you organize and conduct a race. When it's over, write a report on it for the school or local newspaper.

➡ **CHEER HERE! "Ducks" is the official name of a number of sports teams,** including the National Hockey League's Anaheim Ducks, minor league baseball's Long Island (N.Y.) Ducks, and all those of the University of Oregon. Write a cheer that a duck mascot might say to encourage a sports team or player. Develop a dance or movements and perform the cheer.

SIGNS OF THE

I mmigrants in a new country bring their customs and traditions, such as language, dress, and recipes. Germans who settled in Pennsylvania in the late 1600s brought those, plus the practice of painting colorful symbols on circles. These decorations, showing stars, flowers, birds, and hearts in bright colors, appeared on furniture, family Bibles and birth certificates, and quilts and other home goods.

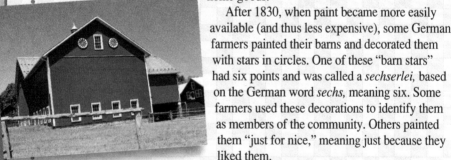

After 1830, when paint became more easily available (and thus less expensive), some German farmers painted their barns and decorated them with stars in circles. One of these "barn stars" had six points and was called a *sechserlei,* based on the German word *sechs,* meaning six. Some farmers used these decorations to identify them as members of the community. Others painted them "just for nice," meaning just because they liked them.

Before long, visitors to the area who were not familiar with the German language or the sign custom confused *sechs* with "hex," the word for a spell cast by a witch. (It didn't help that *Hexe* means "witch" in German!) Soon, people mistakenly began calling the symbols "hex signs." They believed incorrectly that the images and paint colors had special powers. This superstition lasted for years.

Today, nobody believes in the superstitions. People love the signs because they are a colorful and fun way to remind them of the early settlers in the area.

From Deutsch to Dutch

The German word for German is *Deutsch* (pronounced "doy" as in "boy," ending in "t-ch"). Hundreds of years ago, when English-speakers said "Deutsch," it often sounded like they were saying "Dutch." This is why descendants of the earliest German settlers in Pennsylvania are called "Pennsylvania Dutch," even though their ancestors did not come from the Netherlands.

Plain 'n' Fancy

The earliest German emigrants to Pennsylvania belonged to one of two groups:

➡ **The Plain group** included Amish, Mennonites, and others. They settled in southeastern Pennsylvania. Many descendants still speak German at home.

➡ **The Fancy group** included Lutherans and settled in what is now northern Berks county. Their descendants seldom speak German.

TIMES

In this traditional hex sign design, the single goldfinch is a symbol of happiness and good luck. The heart implies love; the tulips, faith.

What's It Mean?

Visitors to Pennsylvania see hex signs on farm buildings and in souvenir shops. These are some of the popular symbols and their meanings:

Chain borders . . . . .long life
Eagles . . . . .courage
Goldfinches . . . . .happiness
Hearts . . . . .love
Oak leaves . . . . .strength
Rabbits . . . . .babies
Scalloped borders . . . . .smooth sailing
Shamrocks . . . . .good luck
Stars with 4 points . . . . .seasons of the year
Sun . . . . .abundance
Unicorns . . . . .plenty

➡ **SIGN UP!** Using these or other symbols, create a barn sign and hang it on a door in your house or on your wall.

ROLLING IN THE

O
A
T
S

Love oatmeal cereal? Crave oatmeal cookies? Hey! What are **OATS?**

A

B

C

D

E

● **OATS** have been around for thousands of years. Seeds were found in Egyptian tombs dating to 2000 B.C. Ancient Romans and Greeks believed that oats were weeds and fed them to farm animals.

● Eventually, people started to realize how tasty and nutritious oats could be. By the year 410, German tribes were filling their bellies with oatcake rations as they invaded the Roman Empire.

◯ Oats were sown in North America before the Pilgrims arrived. In 1602, Captain Bartholomew Gosnold was

exploring the New England coast. On tiny Cuttyhunk Island, in what is now Massachusetts, he planted a few oat grains that he had brought from Europe. Soon, seeds spread to the mainland and oats became a popular crop.

SEE HOW THEY GROW

OATS are a type of grass. Wheat, corn, barley, and rice are grasses, too, but oats are higher in protein and healthy fats than are most other whole grains. Unlike most whole grains, oats grow in cool, rainy places. This is why oats became a popular, reliable crop in Scotland and Ireland.

Species of oats have names such as Large Naked Oat, Small Naked Oat (naked oats don't have hulls), Desert Oat, Sand Oat, and Slender Oat. Varieties include 'Astro', 'Cherokee', 'Clinton', 'Florida 501', 'Noble', and 'Stout'.

Common white oats, called *Avena sativa,* are planted in the spring **A** and harvested in the summer. The stalks grow from 2 to 4 feet high and contain small branches that end in a "spikelet." **B**

Each spikelet contains two seeds that are protected by an outer coating called a "hull," which is too hard for people to eat. Oats in this form are called "whole oats."

Once the hull is removed, the whole grain is called a "groat" (the word is distantly related to "grits"). **Groats C** look like brown rice and can be cooked and eaten.

Groats are often steamed and flattened with a roller into rolled oats. These are softer and cook more quickly than groats. An 18-ounce package of old-fashioned oats contains about 26,000 **rolled oats D**. Rolled oats are commonly used in recipes.

Instant oats are steamed longer and

CONTINUED

rolled to be thinner than rolled oats. However, this additional processing makes them less nutritious than other varieties.

Steel-cut oats are groats that have been cut into three or four pieces. The cutting helps to speed the cooking process. Steel-cut oats are very nutritious and are used to make oatmeal.

TODAY, the world's leading oat growers are the United States, Canada, Russia, Finland, and Poland. People eat oats in many prepared foods, including bacon, beer, bread, breakfast bars, butter, cakes, cereals, cookies, frozen fish, ice cream, meatballs, meat loaf, oat flour, oat milk, salad dressing, and sausage. This accounts for only about 5 percent of the world's oats. The remainder is used for other purposes.

Harvesting oats in Manitoba, Canada

OATS are EVERYWHERE

IN AGRICULTURE

Farm animals often sleep in oat straw and eat oat hay.

OAT NOTES

The term "oatmeal" was probably invented around 1400 to describe flour made from oats.

Draft horses that do the work of tractors often wear nose bags full of oats to eat.

Chickens enjoy eating whole oats. They don't know that the hulls provide them with insoluble fiber—which keeps them from pulling feathers out of one another.

Farmers sometimes use oats as a weed barrier for crops; as ground cover, fertilizer, and mulch; and to control erosion.

IN MEDICINE

Eating oats seems to be helpful in preventing heart disease and cancer and can stabilize blood sugar and lower cholesterol.

Oats have also been used to treat rheumatism, chronic pain, insomnia, stress, anxiety, and depression.

IN COSMETICS

Oats are used in soaps, creams, and gels to stop itchiness or help soothe dry or sunburned skin.

Oats are used in some shampoos and conditioners.

Oats are sometimes used as a home remedy to treat chicken pox, rashes, and acne.

CONTINUED

OAT NOTES

Years ago, the straw part of oat plants that remained after oat grains were harvested was used for drinking straws.

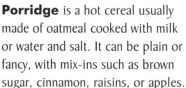

Porridge is a hot cereal usually made of oatmeal cooked with milk or water and salt. It can be plain or fancy, with mix-ins such as brown sugar, cinnamon, raisins, or apples.

In the 18th and 19th centuries, oats were a staple food in Scotland. A favorite dish to this day is called "crowdie," which is made by pouring cold spring water into finely ground oatmeal until the mixture is thin, like pancake batter. It is eaten uncooked.

Today, Carrbridge, Scotland, is the home of the annual World Porridge-Making Championships. The Carrbridge champion wins a Golden Spurtle, a sticklike tool used by Scots for stirring porridge. Scots traditionally eat porridge while standing because "a standing sack fills the fullest."

OAT NOTES

Young people who behave foolishly or badly are sometimes said to have "sown their wild oats." The phrase refers to going wild instead of doing (or, on the farm, growing) something useful.

2011 Porridge champs: specialty winner Neal Robertson, *left,* with John Boa, World Porridge-Making Champion

LOVE IT? LIVE IN IT

OAT fans might consider moving to **Oatmeal, Texas,** founded in 1849 about 36 miles northwest of Austin. The origin of the town name is not what you think. (It is not named for oats.) In fact, the exact origin is not known, but people believe that it's one of these two:

- **The town is named Oatmeal for the owner of the area's first gristmill, Mr. Othneil.**

- **The town name evolved from a translation of "Habermill," the name of a family that lived there around 1849. Haber means "oats" in German dialect.**

Good Things Come in **3**s

In Bertram, Texas (near Oatmeal), a record was set in 1991 on Labor Day. Bertram bakers whipped up the world's largest oatmeal cake. It stood more than **3** feet tall, had **33** layers, weighed **333** pounds, and was tasted by **3,333** people.

OATMEAL ART

Whip up a batch of oatmeal clay and make oatmeal sculptures. This batter is not for eating, but for rolling into beads or other fun shapes or using with cookie cutters.

YOU WILL NEED:

1 cup rolled oats (instant or old-fashioned)
2/3 cup flour
1/2 cup water
food coloring (optional)

Combine all of the ingredients in a large bowl and stir to mix. For colored clay, add a few drops of food coloring to the water before adding it to the flour and oats. The dough will be lumpy. Add more flour—a spoonful at a time—if the dough seems sticky. Dust a countertop with flour. Knead the dough on the floured surface, adding more flour as needed to keep the dough from sticking. Continue until the dough is easy to work and not too sticky. Now you're ready to play with your clay. Allow your masterpieces to dry overnight. Leftover clay can be stored in airtight plastic bags in the refrigerator for a couple of days.

LET'S GO

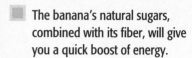

The banana's natural sugars, combined with its fiber, will give you a quick boost of energy.

Research has shown that the potassium in bananas will make you alert.

Eating a banana will reduce stress. It will normalize your heartbeat, send oxygen to your brain, and regulate your body's water balance.

Bananas contain tryptophan, a protein that improves your mood and makes you feel happy.

Bananas are the healthy fruit that makes you happy. They have almost no fat and no cholesterol or sodium. Compared to an apple, the banana has twice the carbohydrates, twice the phosphorus, and four times the protein. Plus, they contain a healthy heaping of vitamin A and double the other vitamins and minerals.

NAS

There are more than 500 different varieties of bananas. They come in many colors, including blue, green, orange, pink, red, and yellow. The super sweet **red bananas** (also called Jamaican bananas) have reddish-purple skin and are grown in South and Central America and on Caribbean islands.

HIGH FIVE!

■ **Bananas grow in bunches (or hands), and each banana is called a finger. Banana is an Arabic word that means "finger."**

■ **The banana "tree" is actually a giant herb. The banana is the fruit of this herb.**

continued ▷

BANANAS are North America's most popular fruit. On average,

THE SKINNY ON BANANA SKINS

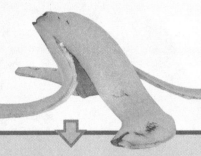

⬇

- Rub scrapes and bruises with the inside of a banana skin. It will promote quick healing.

- Polish your leather shoes with a banana skin. Rub the shoes with the inside of the skin. Then buff with a lint-free cloth.

- Reduce swelling and itching from a bug bite by rubbing the affected area with the inside of a banana skin.

- Place a small piece of banana skin, yellow side out, on a wart. Put a big adhesive bandage over the banana skin to hold it in place. Keep the banana skin on the wart for 1 week to remove the wart.

From Green to Yellow ➡

Can't wait for green bananas to turn yellow? Place the bananas in a paper bag with an apple. Close the bag. Open it in about 24 hours. The ethylene gas in the apple will have caused the bananas to ripen.

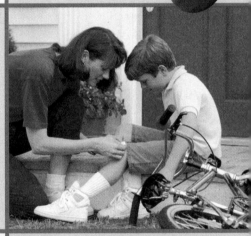

Does This A-Peel TO YOU?

▶ If you peel a banana from the bottom (not the stem end), you won't have to pick the little "stringy things" off of it.

▶ Most monkeys peel bananas by pinching the bottom end of the banana. Try it! The pressure of pinching creates a rip in the peel, and makes it easy to remove.

each person eats about 150 bananas per year (about 26 pounds!).

... and From Yellow to BROWN

A chemical reaction between an enzyme in the fruit and the oxygen in the air causes bananas to turn brown.

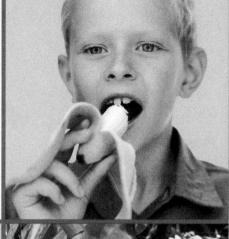

NOT JUST FOR BREAKFAST

String or twine can be made from banana plant fiber, which also can be woven into baskets, place mats, hats, and bags.

The banana plant helps to lower air pollution by absorbing large amounts of carbon dioxide.

Banana leaves are often wrapped around food to be cooked and baked. The leaves can also be used as umbrellas or to polish wooden floors.

The stem of the banana "tree" (really a "pseudostem" made up of the large, overlapping leaf sheaths that form the "trunk") can be used to make rafts and benches. In Sri Lanka, it is made into soles for shoes and used in floor coverings.

continued

On November 19, 2011, Walter Lamerson threw a banana

A Little HISTORY

One of the first mentions of bananas is in Buddhist texts in 600 B.C.

Alexander the Great, king of Macedonia, recorded the first bananas discovered in India in 327 B.C.

Q Why do bananas wear suntan lotion?

A Because they peel!

Almost 28 percent of the bananas in the world are grown and eaten in India. Brazil is the second-biggest source of bananas, followed by China.

Bananas were officially introduced in North America at the 1876 Philadelphia Centennial Exhibition. Each banana was wrapped in foil and sold for 10 cents. Before that, sailors had occasionally brought a few bunches home from the Caribbean.

The banana split was invented in 1904 by 23-year-old David Evans Strickler, an employee at the Tassell Pharmacy soda fountain in Latrobe, Pennsylvania.

Bee Careful! ......

Isoamyl acetate is a banana-scented chemical released by honeybees when they are attacked or angry. It signals other bees to help. The same chemical is found in bananas and gives them their taste. So, don't eat a banana near a beehive or where honeybees are buzzing around.

Why did the banana go to see the doctor?

He was not peeling very well.

• • • • • •

What is Ba + Na$_2$?

Banana

Japanese artist Keisuke Yamada is carving out a unique reputation: He uses a toothpick and a spoon to make sculptures out of bananas. Each one takes about 30 minutes. Keisuke then eats each piece of artwork before it begins to turn brown.

Make Banana-sicles • •

Peel and cut a banana in half (across the middle). Put a wooden ice cream stick into the cut end of each piece. Place the bananas in a plastic bag and put it into the freezer. A few hours later, you'll have sweet frozen banana-sicles. If you like, dip the banana-sicles in melted chocolate before eating!

Twisted Tales

OF THE

WORLD'S OLDEST
SNACK

The exact origins of PRETZELS are unknown . . .

➤ **Around A.D. 600,** monks in southern France (or northern Italy) are said to have baked dough treats called *pretiola* (Latin for "little reward"), shaped like arms bent in prayer. Children received them as a prize for memorizing religious passages.

➤ **As the little reward's popularity spread,** its name changed: In Italy, it became known as *brachiola* ("little arms"). In old German, "little arms" were *brezitella,* which became *bretzel* and eventually "pretzel."

➤ **Some people believe** that the pilgrims who sailed to America on the *Mayflower* brought pretzels with them.

"Pretzel" Language

Denmark	Kringle
France	Le Bretzel
Poland	Precel
Spain	La Rosquilla
Sweden, Switzerland	Kringla
Netherlands	Krakeling

SNACK • FACTS

Centuries ago in Germany on Easter, parents hid pretzels on their family farms and children hunted for them. Eventually, this tradition turned into the Easter egg hunt.

TODAY in Germany on New Year's Day (January 1), pretzels are used as a symbol of good luck. People eat sweet (not salted) pretzels, and grandparents reward their grandchildren with a special pretzel and money.

Pretzel-vania, USA?

- **According to legend,** in the late 1700s in Pennsylvania, an assistant baker fell asleep while his pretzels baked in the oven. He awoke to find that the oven's fire had gone out, so he lit it again. The baking process resulted in the world's first "hard" pretzel. The chief baker is said to have been angry with his assistant—until he tasted the crispy invention.

- **The first U.S. pretzel bakery** opened in Pennsylvania in 1861.

- **The first automatic pretzel-twisting machine** appeared in Pennsylvania in 1947.

- **Today,** Pennsylvania boasts numerous pretzel factories, and pretzel bakeries and street vendors are common in the state capital, Harrisburg.

- **Pretzel Park** in Philadelphia has pretzel-shape paths and a pretzel statue.

 KNOT JOKING

When's the best day to eat pretzels?

 April 26, National Pretzel Day

C O N T I N U E D ■■■▶

Did You Know?

In the United States, pretzels without salt are called baldies.

How Big Can a PRETZEL Be?

26 feet 10 inches long, 10 feet 2 inches wide, 842 pounds.

That's the size of the world's largest pretzel so far, which was produced by two employees of a baking company near Munich, Germany, on September 21, 2008.

How Do You Do the PRETZEL?

With a partner: In a popular swing dance move called the pretzel, two dancers twist their arms in a fancy pattern as their bodies and feet follow.

How Do You Ride a PRETZEL?

Perhaps with your eyes closed. Roller coasters often have a pretzel loop in the track design. The coaster cars and their passengers enter the loop upside down and come out of it on their backs and going backward.

F
O
O
D

What Can You Build With PRETZELS?

A model roller coaster. Busch Gardens, in Williamsburg, Virginia, hosts an annual "Pretzel Coaster Build-Off," challenging contestants to design and build model roller coasters using pretzels and glue.

How Do You Make a PRETZEL?

With your hands! Try this recipe for chewy bread pretzels.

YOU WILL NEED:

- 1½ cups warm water (110° to 115°F)
- 1 package (¼ ounce) active dry yeast
- 1 tablespoon sugar
- 2 teaspoons salt
- 4 cups all-purpose flour
- butter or margarine, for greasing the bowl and baking sheet
- 1 egg, beaten
- coarse salt (optional)

Put the water into a large bowl. Sprinkle the yeast on the water and wait for it to proof, or bubble, 3 to 5 minutes. Add the sugar and salt and stir. Add the flour, 1 cup at a time, stirring after each addition, to form soft dough. Turn the dough onto a lightly floured surface (**A**). With your hands, knead the dough until it is smooth and elastic, about 5 minutes. Smear a large bowl with butter. Place the dough in the bowl, then turn the dough once to get butter on all sides of it. Cover the bowl with a clean dish towel and set it in a warm place to allow the dough to rise. When it has doubled in size, in about 1 hour, remove the towel, make a fist with your hand, and punch the dough once or twice. (This releases the air in it.)

Preheat the oven to 425°F. Grease a cookie sheet. Remove the dough from the bowl and divide it into 15 equal portions. Roll each portion into a 14-inch-long rope (**B**). Shape each rope into a pretzel shape (**C**) and (**D**). After shaping each pretzel, place it on the prepared cookie sheet. Brush the pretzels with the beaten egg and sprinkle with salt, if desired. Cover the pretzels again and set them aside to rise, about 15 minutes. Bake for 15 minutes, or until the color is golden brown. **Makes 15 pretzels.**

(A)

(B)

(C)

(D)

Get Ready, Get Set, GO!

It's time to have a good old-fashioned GAME DAY.

During the last days of summer, folks in many towns in New England celebrate Old Home Day. In 1899, Frank Rollins, then-governor of New Hampshire, came up with the idea as a way to get people who had moved out of state to return "home."

Old Home Day activities can include music recitals, talent shows, parades, dances, town baseball games, and other contests, such as sack races and egg tosses. These games are also easy and fun to play in your backyard. Gather some friends, go outside, and have an old-fashioned game day!

FROG JUMP

Frog jumping is a spectator sport for you, but it's another story for the frog!

You will need:

string or sticks to mark a circle at least
    10 feet in diameter
1 frog per person
ruler or measuring tape

GET READY . . .
Place your frog in the center of the circle and do not touch him again until after his turn.

GET SET . . .
Each player gets one turn, during which his or her frog is allowed three jumps.

GO!
If your frog is shy, you can stomp the ground or clap your hands to get him started.

 REMINDER:
Be sure to wash your hands after holding your frog.

SCORING

- Measure the distance from your frog's starting place to the spot where he lands on his third jump. This distance is his score (example: 3 feet 2 inches). The frog that travels the farthest in three jumps wins.

Variation:

Try frog racing. You will need at least two people. Place your frogs in the center of the circle and shout, "Go!" The first frog to make it to the edge of the circle wins the race.

DID YOU KNOW?

In 1986, during the Jumping Frog Jubilee in Angels Camp, California, the American record for the longest frog jump was set by "Rosie the Ribiter." She traveled 21 feet 5¾ inches in three jumps.

JUMP FOR JOY
May 13 is Frog Jumping Day.

What kind of shoes do frogs wear?

Open-toad!

continued

SACK RACE

Get into this with both feet!

You will need:

2 or more people
1 burlap (potato) sack or large
    pillowcase per person
rope or sticks to mark the start
    and finish lines, about 30
    feet apart

GET READY . . .
Place both feet inside your sack.

GET SET . . .
With both hands, pull your sack
up to your waist. Do not let go.

GO!
Run, stumble, or jump to the
finish line.

SCORING

⬤ The first person across the
finish line wins.

DID YOU KNOW?

Sack racing was once a
serious sport. It was a
competition in the 1904
Olympic Games.

Sack racing has been done
all around the world; even
soldiers have been known to
sack race to pass the time.

3-LEGGED RACE

This is a tricky game that requires teamwork.

You will need:

4 or more people, 2 on each team
1 bandanna or piece of rope per
    team
rope or sticks to mark the start
    and finish lines, about 30 feet
    apart

GET READY . . .
Use a bandanna to tie your
teammate's right ankle to your left
ankle.

GET SET . . .
Stand at the starting line. To keep
your balance, put your left arm
around your teammate's shoulders
and have your teammate put his
right arm around your waist.

WHEELBARROW RACE

It's a 'barrow of fun!

You will need:

4 or more people, 2 on each team
rope or sticks to mark a start and a turnaround line
about 30 feet apart

GET READY...

Decide who will be the wheelbarrow and who will be the driver.

continued ➔

GO!

Run, jump, or hobble with your teammate to the finish line.

SCORING

● The first team to reach the finish line wins.

DID YOU KNOW?

According to Guinness World Records, the largest three-legged race (at a single location) included 502 teams in Ichinomiya, Japan, on November 3, 2011.

GET SET . . .

The "wheelbarrow" gets down on all fours (knees and palms on the ground). The "driver" picks up the wheelbarrow's ankles and extends his or her legs.

GO!

If you're the wheelbarrow, "walk" forward on your hands. If you're the driver, gently push the wheelbarrow forward toward the turnaround line. When you get there, switch positions with your teammate and return to the starting line.

DID YOU KNOW?

According to Guinness World Records, the largest human wheelbarrow race (at a single location) occurred on November 6, 2009, in Armidale, Australia. It consisted of 777 teams.

SCORING

○ The first team to 'barrow back to the starting line wins.

Variation:

Create an obstacle course to "push" the wheelbarrow around. Use common items that will not hurt players if they fall on or against them: beach balls, cardboard boxes, towels spread on the ground.

TRIATHLON

"Tri-" means "three." A triathlon is a race that includes three events— usually swimming, bicycling, and running. Try your own triathlon with a combination of three of the racing events in this article.

GET READY . . .

Pick three events and decide in which order they will be raced. **For example,** start with

EGG-ON-A-SPOON RACE

This is no yoke!

You will need:

2 or more people
1 whole (raw) egg per person
1 spoon per person
rope or sticks to mark the start and finish lines, about 30 feet apart

GET READY . . .
Hold your spoon parallel to the ground with one hand.

GET SET . . .
Balance your egg in the bowl of your spoon.

GO!
Walk or run, carrying the egg in your spoon. If your egg drops and breaks, you're out of the race. If the egg drops but doesn't break, pick it up, go back to the starting line, put it back on your spoon, and continue the race.

SCORING
○ The first person to cross the finish line with a whole egg wins.

DID YOU KNOW?
According to Guinness World Records, the largest egg-on-a-spoon race (at a single location) occurred in Singapore on July 27, 2008, when 1,308 students raced to the finish line.

a sack race, then move to an egg-on-a-spoon segment, then end with a three-legged race.

GET SET . . .
Set up the race course so that each segment ends where it begins (go around some marker and then come back). Place the necessary items (sacks, eggs, spoons, bandannas) at the starting line, which will also be the finish line for each segment. Have a partner waiting for you to begin the three-legged race.

GO!
Start the first segment of the race; once you start, don't stop. When you get to the end of the first race, begin the next segment as quickly as you can.

SCORING
○ The first person or team to cross the finish line of the third event wins.

c o n t i n u e d ➡

EGG TOSS

This game can get messy, so wear clothes that you can get dirty!

You will need:

4 or more people, 2 on each team
1 whole (raw) egg per team

GET READY...

Line up players in two rows 3 feet apart, with teammates standing opposite each other.

GET SET...

Hold your team's egg carefully.

GO!

Throw the egg to your teammate. If he catches it, both of you must take a step backward, increasing the throwing distance for the next toss.

The team that tosses the egg the farthest without breaking it wins.

Variation:

Use water balloons instead of eggs. (This is fun on a hot day!)

DID YOU KNOW?

The seventh World Egg Throwing Championship hosted by the World Egg Throwing Federation took place on June 24, 2012, in Swanton, England.

TUG-OF-WAR

You will need:

2 or more people, separated into 2
   teams
A long, sturdy rope specifically made
   for tugging
1 stick or piece of rope to mark the
   center of the field

GET READY...
Lay the tugging rope across the
stick in the center of the field to
create a cross.

GET SET...
Line up along the length of the
tugging rope, leaving 10 feet
on each side of the center and a
couple of feet between each
person. Pick up the rope and
hold it tightly.

GO!
Pull and tug on the rope as
hard as you can.

SCORING

○ The first team to pull
   the other team across
   the center stick wins.

Variation:

Use a lawn sprinkler or
small, inflatable kiddy pool
as the center line. The first
team to pull the other team
into the water wins.

DID YOU KNOW?

Tug-of-war was an event in the
1900, 1904, 1906, 1908, 1912, and
1920 Olympic Games.

Variations of tug-of-war date
from the ancient Egyptians. It has
been used to strengthen men for
war, occupy dull times, and settle
disputes.

FUN AND GAMES

STEP RIGHT UP, KIDS!

TO · THE GREATEST SHOW ON EARTH!

ADMIT ONE

Years ago, young people who wanted to join the circus ran away from home. Today, kids can go to circus camp, where trained teachers help to develop their skills in a safe environment.

This is how Bekk McGowan and Emma Rogers of New Hampshire joined the circus.

continued ➡

"Activity makes people feel good about themselves," says Bekk. "And circus is the best."

SMIRKUS

They met at the New England Center for Circus Arts (NECCA) in Brattleboro, Vermont, when they were both 14 years old. There they became acrobatic partners. It was a dream that came true after a lot of hard work.

Bekk enjoyed performing as a child and learned to juggle in the 5th grade, but he says that he "didn't get really serious about the circus" until he started doing acrobatics in the 7th grade. Later, he attended a high school that offers circus as part of physical education during and after school. He learned how to ride a unicycle and

Bekk and Emma perform under the Circus Smirkus big top.

"Circus work is really intense, but it allows you to express yourself through something entertaining and rewarding," says Emma.

juggle from a circus trainer and teacher and worked with her and her husband in a circus show.

"I really practice all the time," Bekk says. He means *all the time*. If he's got a few free minutes, such as while waiting for someone in a parking lot, he'll juggle, do headstands, or walk on his hands. "I love it," he adds. "Activity makes people feel good about themselves, and circus is the best. It's really neat to do stuff that most other people can't do."

Emma started juggling early. "I did some when I was really young," she remembers. Later, when she was in junior high school, she saw a performance of Circus Smirkus in Maine, and the energy and enthusiasm of the performers inspired her. "I really wanted to go to the circus," she says. To improve her skills, she participated in competitive gymnastics through the American School of Gymnastics and

continued ➤

studied dance after hours. She had been studying for over 2 years when she was accepted into NECCA.

At circus camps, kids participate in a variety of activities in the morning and on one particular skill in the afternoon. "Circus camp is for all ages and is a great thing to do," Emma enthuses. Reaching the top performance level depends on the student, his or her background, and the activity. At NECCA, Emma worked on acrobatics and aerial fabrics, performing on a kind of curtain suspended from the ceiling. "This is very difficult at first," she says.

After hours of practice together, Bekk and Emma made a video of their act and submitted it to Circus Smirkus, an international youth circus based in Vermont. They were accepted into the program and toured across New England for 6 weeks, helping to set up (including a big tent), put on shows, pack up, and move on to the next town.

Traveling with a circus involves a lot more than just performing. "Kids help with the teardown [taking the tent down and packing it away in the trucks], pick up the trash after a performance, and sell popcorn," Bekk notes. They also work with the riggers, musicians, technicians, and light crew to learn their aspects of the circus. The circus arranges for the kids to stay in private homes, where they meet and make new friends.

For Emma, the circus is a lot of hard work, with a lot of benefits: "I love camp, and I love the circus. Circus work is really intense, but it allows you to express yourself through something entertaining and rewarding." She isn't sure how long she will continue or whether she will make it her career.

Bekk plans to become a professional performer: "There are a lot of circuses around, in addition to the most famous of them all, the Canadian troupe Cirque du Soleil, which is most performers' private goal." It's his goal, too.

ON WITH THE SHOW!

There are many circus camps and schools across the country, with programs that run for a few days or weeks at a time for kids in a range of age groups. Most camps offer all or many of these skills:

Acrobatics (cartwheels, somersaults, handstands, back flips)	Juggling
	Rope climbing
	Tightrope walking
Aerials (on the trapeze and rings)	Timing and teamwork
Baton twirling	Unicycling
Clowning	

BIG TOP

1793

The first circus in America opened in Philadelphia, as part of a riding school, and featured equestrian acts. One of the people in the audience on April 22 was President George Washington. Soon the show was traveling to cities along the East Coast.

1832

American circuses started traveling by train.

1882

Performances were held in three rings for the first time. This allowed everyone in the audience to see some part of the show at all times.

1911

32 circus shows were traveling the country.

1796

The first elephant in America arrived in New York City on April 13.

1800s

Circuses followed pioneers migrating west- and southward.

1825

The big-top canvas circus tent was invented.

GET ON BOARD

Ride the

1000 B.C.	A.D. 1200s	1400s	1900s

The first surfers were likely Peruvian fishermen who rode the waves to bring their catch to shore.

The people of western Polynesia brought modern surfing, as well as *paipo* (belly) boarding, to the islands now known as Hawaii. Men, women, and children all participated.

Surfing was perfected in Hawaii. There, during the 15th century, locals called the sport *he'e nalu*. *He'e* means to change from solid to liquid form, and *nalu* refers to wave motion.

In 1912, Duke Paoa Kahanamoku, one of Hawaii's best swimmers, caused a sensation when he performed surfing demonstrations in southern California.

Duke introduced surfing to Australia in 1915, when he made an 8-foot 6-inch surfboard from native Australian sugar pine. When he rode the board at Freshwater Beach in Manly, he started a surfing frenzy.

Duke Kahanamoku

Surf

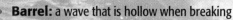

- **Barrel:** a wave that is hollow when breaking
- **Carve:** to turn on a wave
- **Ding:** damage to a surfboard
- **Duck dive:** a dive under a wave when paddling out
- **Fakie:** to ride a surfboard backward, or tail first
- **Hang ten:** to ride a long board with both feet on the nose of the board
- **Locked in:** when a wave crashes and the surfer is inside of it
- **Mullering:** a big wipe out
- **Slash:** a rapid turn off the top of the wave
- **Stick:** slang for a surfboard

1920s

Interest in surfing grew in California. Swimmers mostly used boards made from heavy redwoods and hardwoods.

1930s–'40s

Surfboard builders experimented with sizes, shapes, weights, and materials. For example, they tried waterproof glues instead of bolts to hold the board together. They added a small fin to the underside of the board. This helped in turning and cutting through the waves. They eventually made the boards of fiberglass, resin, and Styrofoam.

1950s+

Californians went crazy for surfing, with heavy balsa and redwood boards. In 1959, a book and a movie about a surfer girl named Gidget made the sport popular among girls.

Actress Sally Field in TV's 1965 *Gidget* program

TODAY

Surfing is a popular sport around the world.

continued · · · · · · · · ·▶

Ride the Slopes

1939	1965	1970s–80s	1982

Vern Wicklund and brothers Harvey and Gunnar Burgeson patented the Sno-Surf. They described the use of their invention as being like surfing on snow and an alternative to skiing.

The Sno-Surf

On December 25, Sherman Poppen of Muskegon, Michigan, invented the Snurfer (think "snow surfer") for his kids. He tied together two skis and added some cross braces about 6 inches apart so that feet could be held in place.

SNURFING!
the greatest word in downhill fun since YAHOOOooooooooo!

the thrills of SKIING! the skills of SURFING!

Snurfer

Brunswick

As snowboarding became more popular, pioneers, including Dimitrije Milovich, an East Coast surfer, and Jake Burton Carpenter from Vermont, developed new board designs.

The first international snowboard race was held at Suicide Six, a ski area near Woodstock, Vermont. The course was a steep, icy downhill run called "The Face."

- **Bonk:** bouncing off an object such as a rock, tree, or stump
- **Eat:** wiping out
- **Half pipe:** a U-shape bowl of snow that boarders traverse and in which they jump and turn
- **Jib:** sliding on nonsnow surfaces such as rails or platforms with the snowboard
- **Ollie:** a jump using the tail of the snowboard as a spring
- **Regular foot:** riding with the left foot forward on the snowboard
- **Slopestyle:** a freestyle competition in which participants are judged on tricks performed on jumps and other structures
- **Spinal tap:** equivalent to a backward face plant, in which you fall hard on your back after catching your heel edge
- **Tabletop:** a mound of snow with the top sheared off to provide a flat, level landing area
- **Whoop de doos:** a grouping of elongated bumps

1985	**1990–92**	**1998**

Only 39 of about 600 U.S. ski resorts allowed snowboards. Lots of skiers and snowboarders collided on the slopes, resulting in broken boards and skis, broken bones, and a lot of bruises.

Farmer Doug Waugh created the Pipe Dragon, a piece of farm machinery that cut large "half-pipes" out of big snow piles.

Snowboarding became an Olympic sport at the games in Nagano, Japan.

TODAY

Snowboarding is the fastest-growing winter sport in the United States.

A Pipe Dragon at work

Put Your Best FOOT

E ach of us has a unique pattern of walking, called a gait. Each leg has a gait cycle:

■ **"Stance" is the period during which one foot is on the ground, supporting the body.**

■ **"Swing" is the period during which that foot is off the ground.**

When one leg begins its gait cycle, the other is about halfway through. At the same time, your arms, hips, and other parts of your body also help to move you forward.

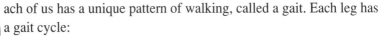

Did You Know?

➡ **We learn to walk usually between 9 and 15 months of age.**

➡ **To walk 1 mile at a normal pace, a person takes 2,000 steps, on average. A normal walking pace is about 3 to 4 mph.**

➡ **No two people walk in exactly the same way.**

FORWARD

All in Stride

- A STEP length is the distance between the footstep of one foot and the footstep of the other foot.

- A STRIDE length is the distance between two footsteps of the same foot. (There are two steps in one stride.)

The Way to WALK

Many of us do not walk correctly. One reason is poor posture. Good posture allows us to breathe easily, concentrate, avoid health complications, and feel good about ourselves.

CONTINUED

TRY THIS:

TRY THIS:

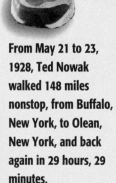

1

STAND IN FRONT OF A MIRROR
- Position your body in a straight line from earlobe, shoulder, and hip. (Imagine that someone is pulling you up by your head!)
- Keep your back straight, not arched or slumped.
- Set your shoulders slightly back and down.

2

START WALKING
- Avoid leaning forward or backward; this will strain your muscles.
- Keep your chin parallel to the ground. Focus on an area about 15 feet in front of you. (To look down, lower your eyes, not your head.)
- Point your feet and knees forward; try not to angle them.
- Relax—do not be rigid!

3

FEEL THE HEEL
- Touch the ground with your heel, not the entire foot or the toes or the ball (the padded area between the arch of your foot and the toes).
- Roll the foot forward, ending with the big toe. (The heel will rise.)
- Push off with the toes.

FOOT NOTES

From May 21 to 23, 1928, Ted Nowak walked 148 miles nonstop, from Buffalo, New York, to Olean, New York, and back again in 29 hours, 29 minutes.

• • •

From December 31, 1989, to January 1, 1990, in Minneapolis, Minnesota, Anthony Thornton walked 95.7 miles backward in 23 hours, 45 minutes.

• • •

On February 26, 2011, at the Russian Winter Racewalking Championships in Sochi, Vera Sokolova racewalked 20 kilometers (about 12.5 miles) in 1 hour, 25 minutes, 8 seconds.

FAST TRACK

Speed- or power-walking is a fitness and weight-loss technique. Walkers travel at about 4.5 to 5 mph.

TRY IT!

Relax shoulders and arms; bend your arms at a 90-degree angle.

Start walking: Use shorter strides than normal but take more steps.

Loosely cup your hands and swing your arms from the shoulders forward and back, close to your body. Your hands should go no higher than your chest and no farther back than your hips.

FASTER TRACK

Racewalking can be done at any pace, but some athletes travel faster than 9 mph. It is similar to speed-walking but has specific rules:

1 You must keep in contact with the ground at all times: Before the toes of your back foot lift off the ground, the heel of your front foot must touch the ground.

2 You must straighten your front leg when the front heel contacts the ground and keep the leg straight until it becomes vertical and passes directly under the body. After that, you can bend it at the knee and eventually move it forward to take the next step.

TO INCREASE SPEED AND ENDURANCE, RACEWALKERS . . .

- Always push off hard with the toes.
- Walk so that all steps fall into a nearly straight line.
- Keep the rear foot in contact with the ground as long as possible.
- Keep the leg straight until the heel lifts off the ground in the back.
- Keep the foot as close to the ground as possible when moving the back leg to the front.
- Rotate the hips forward and back, rather than side to side.

A Most Unlucky Day

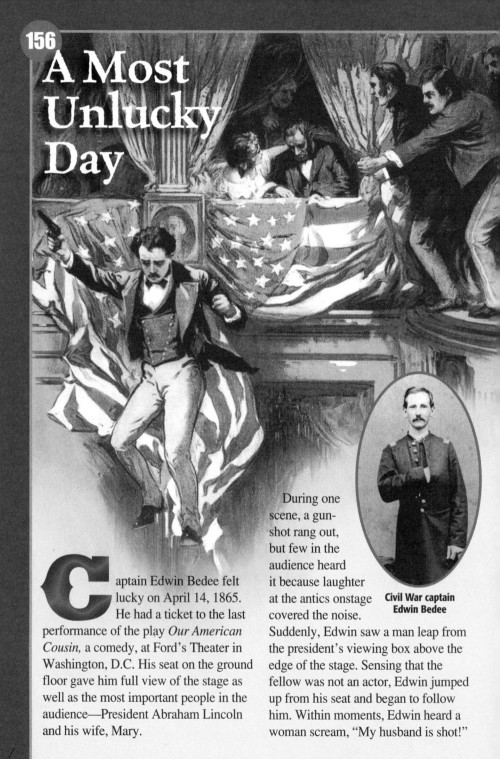

Civil War captain
Edwin Bedee

Captain Edwin Bedee felt lucky on April 14, 1865. He had a ticket to the last performance of the play *Our American Cousin,* a comedy, at Ford's Theater in Washington, D.C. His seat on the ground floor gave him full view of the stage as well as the most important people in the audience—President Abraham Lincoln and his wife, Mary.

During one scene, a gunshot rang out, but few in the audience heard it because laughter at the antics onstage covered the noise. Suddenly, Edwin saw a man leap from the president's viewing box above the edge of the stage. Sensing that the fellow was not an actor, Edwin jumped up from his seat and began to follow him. Within moments, Edwin heard a woman scream, "My husband is shot!"

That woman was Mary Lincoln.

All of the actors froze, the audience went silent, and a few people tried to enter the president's box to give aid, but the door was wedged shut from the inside.

A doctor tried to climb into the president's box from the stage, and Edwin ran to help him. Then Edwin himself climbed into the box. He held President Lincoln's head in his hands as the doctor, searching for a bullet wound, removed the president's jacket. The movement of the clothing caused some papers to fall from the jacket's pockets. Mary Lincoln handed the papers to Edwin. She removed other documents from the jacket's pockets and handed them to Edwin, too.

The doctor, Edwin, and several other men carried the ailing president to a house across the street, where he died early the next morning. When the secretary of war arrived, Edwin gave the papers to him, signing his name and regiment on the wrapper that was placed around the bundle. The secretary then told Edwin to send a message to the War Department and alert the authorities to the fugitive who had leaped from the box.

After completing both tasks, the secretary thanked Edwin for his diligence, and told him to return to his post.

The next evening, Edwin was arrested as a suspect in the assassination of President Lincoln! Edwin fretted in jail for 2 long days until the truth came out. A low-ranking officer had become confused about the connections between Edwin, the president's papers,

and the assassination and believed that Edwin had committed the murder.

When he was released, Edwin wrote a letter to the secretary of war. In it, he expressed distress that his honorable record was now tarnished. The secretary wrote back, indicating that he would clear Edwin's name, and he praised Edwin for his role in dealing with the tragic events of that day.

One month later, Edwin was promoted to major. John Wilkes Booth was subsequently identified as the man who had assassinated Abraham Lincoln.

In His Pockets

When Abraham Lincoln was assassinated, his pockets held these items, which now reside in the U.S. Library of Congress:

➡ two pairs of spectacles and a lens polisher

➡ a pocketknife

➡ a watch fob

➡ a linen handkerchief

➡ a brown leather wallet containing a five-dollar Confederate note

➡ nine newspaper clippings about the president and his policies

LIBERTY

The Statue of Liberty was conceived as a gift from the people of France to the people of the United States soon after the end of the U.S. Civil War in 1865. It was to be a sign of the long friendship between the two countries and a symbol of liberty and freedom.

Visitors view New York Harbor from the torch.

Frédéric-Auguste Bartholdi (1834–1904), a sculptor who was fascinated by colossal projects, was chosen to design the statue. He hoped that it would be completed for the 100th anniversary of American independence in 1876. However, by that year, only the hand and torch had been finished.

On October 28, 1886, the Statue of Liberty was unveiled in New York Harbor.

In 1882, workers construct the statue in Frédéric's Parisian workshop.

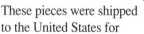

Frédéric-Auguste Bartholdi

In 1884, the completed statue stands outside the foundry in Paris while the base is being constructed in New York.

These pieces were shipped to the United States for display during the centennial celebrations. When the head was finished 2 years later, it was displayed at a park in Paris.

Frédéric and a team of helpers worked 10-hour days, 7 days a week, for 9 years to create the statue. One of the most important members of the team was Alexandre Gustave Eiffel, who later designed the Eiffel Tower. He developed the inner iron framework to support the statue.

On March 3, 1877, President Ulysses S. Grant designated Bedloe's Island (now called Liberty Island) in New York Harbor as the statue's official site. Such a large and heavy object could not sit simply on the soil. A base was needed. Construction of the statue's base began in 1883, with the digging of a 15-foot-deep hole for a foundation.

In the meantime, the statue was finished in France. The pieces were packed in 214 wooden boxes and placed on board the frigate *Isère*.

continued

Rough seas nearly sank the ship, but it safely arrived in New York on June 17, 1885, to cheering crowds and a parade. Because the pedestal (base) was not ready, the boxes were put in storage.

Looking up through the interior framework of the Statue of Liberty

When the concrete-and-granite pedestal was finished in 1886, it had walls up to 20 feet thick. Workers threw silver coins into the final layer of mortar for luck.

Installation of the statue on the site began almost immediately. Finally, on October 28, 1886, Frédéric released a French flag that had been draped over the face of his creation 8 days earlier, and the Statue of Liberty was unveiled to the public.

From Head to Toe

- From her heel to the top of her head, the Statue of Liberty is 111 feet 6 inches tall.

- From the ground to the tip of the flame, the statue measures 305 feet 6 inches. When it was unveiled, the statue was the tallest structure in New York.

- The statue's crown has seven rays, one for each of the seven continents and seven seas.

- The Statue of Liberty is covered in copper that is $3/32$ of an inch thick. That's less than the thickness of two pennies put together.

Light Switches

The torch has been repaired or replaced several times. The newest one, installed in 1986, has a flame that is covered in thin sheets of 24-karat gold. The original torch is on display in the monument's lobby.

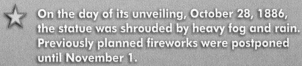

Does the Lady Need an Umbrella?

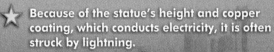

⭐ On the day of its unveiling, October 28, 1886, the statue was shrouded by heavy fog and rain. Previously planned fireworks were postponed until November 1.

⭐ Because of the statue's height and copper coating, which conducts electricity, it is often struck by lightning.

⭐ In August 1933, an electrical storm extinguished the statue's torch.

⭐ The statue can sway up to 3 inches in strong winds, while the torch can move up to 6 inches during 50-mph gusts. The strongest wind may have occurred on October 14, 1954, when the National Weather Service recorded winds of 113+ mph in New York City.

⭐ The statue's copper coating has been exposed to years of rain and snow, causing a chemical reaction and creating a film that has changed the statue's original copper color to light green. This new coating is called a "patina."

STICK WITH IT

The Statue of Liberty (or portions of it) has appeared on at least 50 U.S. **postage stamps.** Worldwide, it has appeared on about 650 stamps representing more than 100 nations.

 continued

PADDLE to Liberty

Since 1996, the Hawaiian Airlines Liberty Challenge hosted by New York Outrigger, a race of Hawaiian-style outrigger canoes in New York's Hudson River, has been held annually. Challenged occasionally by bad weather and rough water, tidal currents, and other boats, teams complete a 15-mile course that passes by the statue.

SWIM Around Liberty

Since 2008, the Statue of Liberty Swim has attracted qualified swimmers to dive into the waters at Liberty Island and swim ¾ of a mile around it in a counterclockwise direction.

She Walks, She Talks!

It is said that sculptor Frédéric Bartholdi used his mother, Charlotte, as a model for the statue's face. He could have used Jennifer Stewart's face.

When Jennifer was a teacher, one of her students told her that she looked like the Statue of Liberty. A year later, on the statue's 100th anniversary, Jennifer entered a national Statue of Liberty Look-Alike Contest. She painted her skin green with water-based paint, donned a draping green gown, adapted a floor mop for a torch, and used plaster and an old laundry basket to create a crown.

Jennifer's costume was so convincing that she won the contest! Since then, she has made a career of "playing" the Statue of Liberty at public events, business meetings, and in advertisements. When she poses and doesn't move (which she says she can do for up to 20 minutes), people do not realize that she is not a statue.

MAKE WAY FOR CAMELS

These "ships of the desert" sailed into—and then out of— U.S. military history.

Explorers in Death Valley first proposed using camels instead of mules as transport in the 1830s. This seemed like a good idea because . . .

Jefferson Davis

■ **Camels are herbivorous and eat desert plants that other animals find inedible.**

■ **Camels tolerate hot weather.**

■ **One camel can carry more than six mules can.**

■ **Camels travel twice as fast as mules.**

Franklin Pierce

In 1855, U.S. Secretary of War Jefferson Davis wanted to use camels instead of horses for the U.S. Army in the Southwest for many of the same reasons. Davis needed Congress to fund his plan. Eventually, it did. The camels were in northern Africa and the Middle East. To transport them to the United States, the cargo ship USS *Supply* was equipped with hay-lined stalls below deck. There, the camels would be tied down so that they would not break their legs during stormy weather. Holes were cut into the upper deck for the camels' humps to poke out.

CONTINUED ⇨

The USS *Supply* returned from Turkey in April 1856 with 34 camels, including one calf born at sea.

Crowds gathered to watch as the camel drivers commanded the animals to kneel, rise, and walk. One woman clipped enough camel hair to knit a pair of socks, which she later sent to President Franklin Pierce. Forty-one more camels arrived in February 1857.

Soldiers found the camels to be ornery creatures that smelled foul, had bad breath, and slobbered on and bit them. And, the camels were very different from horses: The camels ate the cactus fences that served as their corral. When a saddled camel ran at full speed, the soldier riding it often suffered motion sickness from the pitching.

In 1858, 25 camels, with soldiers and drivers, traveled from Camp Verde, Texas, to Fort Tejon, California, and back again as a test of their resiliency and usefulness. The trip was so successful that some men began talking about having camels

FLYING CAMELS ⇨

During World War I (1914–18), pilots flew fighter aircraft called Sopwith Camels. The nickname came from the biplane's maker, Sopwith Aviation Company in England, and the hump that covered its machine guns.

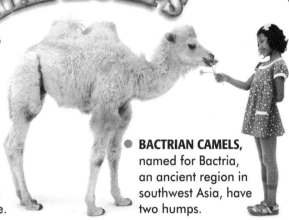

- **ARABIAN CAMELS,** also called dromedaries, have one hump.

- Camels store fat, not water, in their humps, which have a capacity of up to 80 pounds. Camels convert the fat in their humps to energy when food and water are not available.

- **BACTRIAN CAMELS,** named for Bactria, an ancient region in southwest Asia, have two humps.

deliver mail. One official in Washington said that they could be used for military operations in the Great Plains. He wanted the government to buy 1,000 more!

None of those things happened. The country was on the verge of the Civil War, and Jefferson Davis became the leader of the Confederacy. He and others in government and the military, as well as the citizenry, focused their attention on slavery and secession.

As interest in the camels faded, some of them were sold to transport supplies to western mines. A few went to circuses and zoos. Many were turned loose in the Arizona and California deserts.

Today, in Quartzsite, Arizona, a monument stands in tribute to the camel corps—which formed the only camel train in U.S. history. The 10-foot-high pyramid, with a camel on top, stands over the grave of chief camel driver Hadji Ali (whose nickname was "Hi Jolly"). Legend has it that inside the pyramid are the ashes of Topsy, the last camel to trek across the deserts of the Southwest.

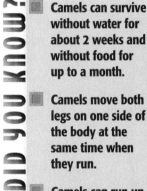

DID YOU KNOW?

- Camels can survive without water for about 2 weeks and without food for up to a month.

- Camels move both legs on one side of the body at the same time when they run.

- Camels can run up to 40 mph in short bursts and up to 25 mph at a constant gait.

- The life span of a camel ranges from 30 to 60 years, on average.

- Camel wool is used to make clothing, tents, and blankets.

FLOAT ALONG

"The Big Muddy"

What has five "eyes" and runs more than 2,000 miles?

THE MISSISSIPPI RIVER

☞ This beloved river begins at Lake Itasca, Minnesota, and flows about 2,340 miles before releasing its waters into the Gulf of Mexico. Along the way, it passes through 10 states, providing endless economic and natural resources, recreation, and a boatload of tales.

NUMBER 4 IN THE WORLD . . .

Among the world's longest rivers:

1. **NILE** (4,160 miles)
2. **AMAZON** (4,000 miles)
3. **YANGTZE RIVERS** (3,964 miles)
4. **MISSISSIPPI–MISSOURI RIVERS** (3,710 miles)

RULER, PLEASE!

■ Measuring the length of rivers is a tricky business. River conditions are constantly changing, affected by factors such as flooding, erosion, and more.

As a result, measurements differ from time to time. Various sources report the Mississippi River as being from 2,320 to about 2,350 miles long.

ONE VERY LONG NAME

It's fun to spell the name of this river quickly, but where did this name originate?

It comes from the Ojibwe Native American words *mishi* for "great" and *sibi* for "river."

VERY MANY SHORT NAMES

In story, song, and lore, the Mississippi has been called Ol' Man River, Old Blue, The Big Muddy, the Father of Waters, and the Gathering of Waters.

• • •

KEY TO THE MAP

1 **Minneapolis**
2 **Hannibal**
3 **Camp Wood**
4 **Cahokia**
5 **St. Louis**
6 **Memphis**
7 **New Orleans**

CONTINUED

ABOUT A.D. 750 TO 800:

A Mysterious City

An ancient Native American settlement called Cahokia **4** was started where the Illinois, Mississippi, and Missouri rivers meet. Cahokia boasted 120 mounds of earth with wooden houses on top, where city leaders lived, and 10,000 to 20,000 residents. Around 1250, Cahokia was the largest city north of Mexico, but by 1492, it had become virtually abandoned. No one knows where all of these people went, but some of the mounds remain near St. Louis, Missouri.

A painting depicts the Cahokia settlement in Illinois.

☞ To find numbered locations, see the map on page 167.

1541:

First Sighting, Last Stop

Spanish explorer Hernando de Soto *(below)* is believed to have been the first European to see the Mississippi, but he probably wasn't happy about it. He had to get

several hundred of his men across while avoiding hostile Native Americans. One year later, Hernando went into the river again; his body was dumped there after he died from a fever.

1673:

A Mississippi Monster?

French missionary Jacques Marquette and French-Canadian fur trader Louis Joliet hoped to find a passage to the Pacific Ocean and to claim land for France. With five others, they set off

in birch bark canoes to explore. The first surprise? Marquette looked into the water and saw "a monster

with the head of a tiger, the nose of a wildcat, and whiskers." (It was probably a catfish.)

1790s:

Navigating Main Street

Boats of all shapes and sizes, built to carry all kinds of businesses—fruit and vegetable stands, blacksmiths' and tinners' shops, theater companies, circuses, and taverns—traveled the river as if it were a road. Before long, pirates prowled the waterway and its shores.

1804:

A Monumental Journey Begins

Meriwether Lewis and William Clark *(below)* spent the fall and winter of 1803–04 at Camp Wood **3**, on Wood River, upstream from St. Louis **5**, recruiting and training a team to explore the lands west of the Mississippi. On May 14, 1804, the group set out from the mouth of the Missouri River in a

big boat with 10 tons of supplies, two smaller boats, and Seaman, Meriwether's Newfoundland dog.

1811:

Churning the Waters

The first steamboat to navigate the Mississippi and one of its tributaries, the Ohio River, was *New Orleans*, which departed from Pittsburgh on October 20, 1811, and arrived in New Orleans **7** on January 12, 1812.

MID-1800s:

Hometown Heroes

Samuel Clemens *(below)* grew up swimming, fishing, and playing pirates in

the port town of Hannibal, Missouri **2**. Despite his love for the river, it nearly killed him. In his autobiography, he wrote: "I was drowned seven times . . . before I learned to swim—once in Bear Creek and six times in the Mississippi." He became a river pilot in 1858 and later an author using the pen name "Mark Twain," a term used to indicate that a section of the river was 2 fathoms' deep, enough for a boat to travel. He based

the tales of his characters Tom Sawyer and Huck Finn on his experiences.

1865:

Disaster!

On April 27, the steamboat SS *Sultana*, dangerously overloaded, was traveling upriver near Memphis, Tennessee **6**. At 2:00 A.M., its boilers exploded, causing the death of up to 1,800 of its more than 2,000 passengers, making it the worst maritime disaster in U.S. history.

The overloaded SS *Sultana*, on the day before its boilers exploded

CONTINUED

1870:

A Long-Distance Race

On June 30, steamboats named *Robert E. Lee* and *Natchez*, both about 300 feet long, began a race

from New Orleans 7 to St. Louis 5—1,278 river miles. Both ships experienced mechanical problems along the way, but *Robert E. Lee* won the event on July 4, in a time of 3 days, 18 hours, 14 minutes.

1874:

Bridging a Great Nation

On July 4, the first steel suspension bridge in the

world, the Eads Bridge, opened, joining St. Louis 5 with the West. Named for its designer, former river pilot James Buchanan Eads, the bridge is still in use.

1922:

A Speedy Sport

On July 2, 18-year-old Ralph Samuelson *(below)* strapped wooden planks

to his feet and, with a long window sash as a tow rope, had his brother tow him behind a speedboat on Lake Pepin, Minnesota, the largest lake along the Mississippi River. It was the first successful attempt at waterskiing.

☞ To find numbered locations, see the map on page 167.

1965:

A New View

On October 28, construction was completed on the tallest monument in the United States, the 630-foot Gateway Arch on the bank of the river in St. Louis 5. The arch honors people who pioneered the West (visitors to the observation deck at the top have east- and west-facing views) and is built to sway up to 18 inches in bad weather. (It takes a 50-mph wind to move the top 1½ inches.)

The Gateway Arch overlooks the Mississippi River in St. Louis.

1993:

Really Big Muddy

The worst flooding in modern history occurred from April to October on the Mississippi:

☞ 47 people died

☞ 9 states were affected

☞ 75 towns were covered with water

☞ 20+ million acres flooded

☞ 54,000 people were evacuated

☞ 50,000 homes were destroyed

2002:

Marathon Man

Marathon swimmer Martin Strel became the first person to swim the length of the Mississippi River. He began in Lake Itasca on July 4 and swam for 68 days, finishing on September 9 at the Mississippi River delta in Louisiana. Along the way, he dealt with alligators, pollution, waves, a whirlpool, and even a lightning bolt.

2007:

Catastrophe!

On August 1, in the evening, part of an interstate bridge across the Mississippi near

Minneapolis, Minnesota, **1** collapsed. Several vehicles fell into the water; 13 people were killed and many more were injured. The bridge was being repaired at the time.

2011:

One Stroke at a Time

On September 9, British adventurer Dave Cornthwaite *(below)* became the first person to have traveled the length of the Mississippi aboard

a stand-up paddleboard, earning the nickname "Stand Up Huck"(a nod to Huck Finn, who rafted down the river). Dave began his 82-day expedition on June 19 in Lake Itasca, taking an estimated 1.3 million strokes along the way.

HOW TO
FEED a PET
its FOOD . . .

1 Train your pet to sit politely for treats, not to jump and dive or grab to get the treat.

Stephanie C.'s dog was not trained to sit for food. "I still have a scar on my thumb from a bite that I got from trying to feed a bulldog puppy a waffle," she says. Like many dogs, Stephanie's puppy was probably rewarded occasionally when it jumped for things it wanted. When she offered a really special treat, the dog did what came naturally.

2 Hold the food or treat properly in your hand.

When food is given by hand, the position of your hand is important. Horses and donkeys should be fed with flat palms. Kittens under 8 to 10 weeks old should be fed with the treat extended past the fingertips or on a spoon; kittens are especially bad at telling where a hand starts

. . . and NOT your

and food ends. Paula L. was bitten by a cat while using a slice of bologna to try to coax it out from under a horse trailer. "Lesson learned: Do not lay lure across fingertips," she notes.

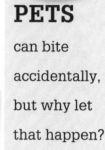

PETS

can bite accidentally, but why let that happen?

3 When handling a pet, be sure that your hands do not smell of its food, especially if the pet relies primarily on smell to find its food or if the pet has bad eyesight.

Francis D. was bitten by his milk snake when he forgot to wash his hands after handling the snake's food (a frozen mouse) and before picking up the snake. "So he associated the heat of my hand and the smell of the mouse and thought it was food," Francis reports.

If you have a pet and have trained it to eat or sit or do other things, share your tips at **Almanac4kids.com/TellUs.**

FINGERS!

Animal memorials are more than just pet projects.

LARGER Than LIFE

At the Cincinnati Zoo in Ohio, a bronze sculpture and pagoda-style building that was used as a bird aviary honors the **last known passenger pigeon, Martha.** Passenger pigeons were once the most numerous birds on Earth and could

A **bronze cow** stands between statues of Mother Teresa and Mahatma Gandhi at the Peace Abbey in Sherborn, Massachusetts. It marks the grave of a 1,600-pound bovine named Emily that made quite a stir in Hopkinton, Massachusetts, in 1995 when she escaped from a slaughterhouse by jumping a fence. Aided by townspeople who stopped alerting police to her whereabouts, Emily eluded capture for 40 days. She eventually found a permanent home at the Peace Abbey in Sherborn and became a "spokescow" for a vegetarian diet. Emily died in 2003, and in 2005, her resting place was officially dedicated as the Sacred Cow Animal Rights Memorial.

fly faster than a mile a minute. Martha died at the zoo in 1914; her memorial, known as the Passenger Pigeon Memorial, is a national historic landmark. As a result of the birds' extinction, conservation laws have been put into effect to save many other species.

An 8-foot-high **fiberglass jackrabbit** in Odessa, Texas, recognizes the area's large jackrabbit population. A marker beside it commemorates the World's First Championship Jackrabbit Roping, staged during the 1932 Odessa Rodeo. (Ropings have since been banned due to pressure from the Humane Society.)

CONTINUED • • • •➤

A slightly oversize **bronze statue of a U.S. soldier and his "war dog"** stands at the New Jersey Vietnam Veterans Memorial in Holmdel, New Jersey. War dogs are trained in teams to patrol and to scout, track, and detect enemy forces. This first official war dog memorial honors canines that have served in the U.S. armed forces since World War I.

Harborside in Rockport, Maine, a **marble harbor seal** named Andre lounges on a rock. The real Andre spent his winters at the New England Aquarium in Boston, Massachusetts, and was released into Boston harbor every spring for more than 20 years. He would then swim to Rockport, where he entertained locals and summer tourists. Andre was Maine's most famous summer visitor before his death in 1986.

A **white marble baby elephant** marks the grave of William F. Duggan in Moultrie, Georgia. William grew up in Moultrie dreaming of joining the circus. His wish came true at age 13, when he became the water boy for a herd of circus elephants. He never lost

At Kentucky Horse Park in Lexington, Kentucky, a **massive bronze horse** perches above the tomb of Man o' War, a famous racehorse in the first half of the 20th century. Some say that he was the greatest thoroughbred racehorse of all time. Man o' War was quite a tourist attraction, too. People from all over the country came to see him at his farm. In 1947, 2,000 people attended his funeral, and the ceremony was broadcast over the radio.

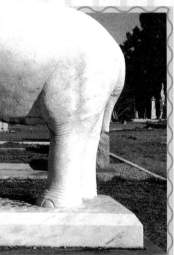

New Mexico's state bird is the roadrunner, so it is only fitting to find the **world's largest roadrunner** in Las Cruces. But this is no ordinary big bird. It is about 20 feet high and made entirely of trash recovered from the city dump. Its belly is crafted of discarded shoes, and the remainder of the bird is made up of everything from office fans to steering wheels to children's toys.

his passion for pachyderms, even when years later he became the owner of the Hagen-Wallace Circus. The 5½-foot-high statue honors William's dream, accomplishment, and lifelong love.

Can You Top That?

What other animal commemorations have you seen? Tell other kids all about them at Almanac4kids.com/TellUs.

FAST FACTS*

NATURE

FASTEST Reptile

The leatherback sea turtle.

22 mph

Although these reptiles move slowly on land, their big front flippers make them fast underwater swimmers.

FASTEST Land Animal

The cheetah.

Sarah, an 11-year-old cheetah at the Cincinnati Zoo in Ohio, set a new land-speed record on June 20, 2012, by running 109 yards in 5.95 seconds, a sprint during which she was clocked at 61 mph!

61 mph

FASTEST Flying Insect

90 mph

The horsefly.

Compare its speed to that of a housefly, whose top speed is only 4.5 mph.

68 mph

FASTEST Fish

The sailfish.

(*Istiophorus platypterus*), which can weigh up to 220 pounds.

FASTEST Creature on Earth

The peregrine falcon.

When this bird dives for its prey, it "falls" out of the sky at speeds that no other bird or animal can match.

200 mph

* These fast facts were accurate when these pages were produced. Let us know of fast facts in any other category or any that are faster than these at **Almanac4kids.com/TellUs.**

MACHINES

350 mph

FASTEST
Motorcycle

The Dodge Tomahawk.

It uses a simple 2-speed manual transmission system.

FASTEST
Two-Legged Robot

6.8 mph

MABEL,

a two-legged robot that was built at the University of Michigan in 2008, has knees that enable it to walk and run like a human.

FASTEST
Roller Coaster

Formula Rossa

at Ferrari World, which opened on October 27, 2010, in Abu Dhabi in the United Arab Emirates. It goes from 0 to 149 mph in 4 seconds.

149 mph

128 mph

FASTEST
Roller Coaster in North America

Kingda Ka

at Six Flags Great Adventure opened on May 21, 2005, in Jackson, New Jersey. It goes from 0 to 128 mph in 3.5 seconds.

FASTEST Car

The 2011 Bugatti Veyron Super Sport

is the world's fastest car that can be driven legally on the street (as well as on a racetrack). It costs about $2.5 million.

267 mph

CONTINUED

SPORTS

FASTEST
Downhill Skateboarder
Mischo Erban

80.83 mph

of Vernon, British Columbia. He set this record skating down a hill in northern Colorado on October 24, 2010.

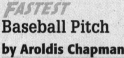

FASTEST
Baseball Pitch
by Aroldis Chapman

105.1 mph

of the Cincinnati Reds. He set this Major League Baseball record with his fastball thrown on September 24, 2010.

FASTEST
Ice Hockey Slap Shot
by Denis Kulyash

of Russia's Kontinental Hockey League. He set this world record at a KHL all-star game in St. Petersburg, Russia, on February 5, 2011.

110 mph

JUST

FASTEST
Tennis Serve
163.4 mph

by Sam Groth

from Australia. He set this record in South Korea on May 9, 2012. (He hit two other record-breaking serves in the same match!)

FASTEST
Dog to Unwind a Nonelectric Car Window
11.34 seconds:

Striker,

a border collie. He set this record in Quebec City, Quebec, on September 1, 2004.

FASTEST
Dog to Pop 100 Balloons
44.49 seconds:

Anastasia,

a Jack Russell terrier. She set this record in Los Angeles, California, on February 24, 2008.

FASTEST
Human Crab Walker
7.84 seconds:

Cameron Jones

from Issaquah, Washington. He set this record by crab walking 65 feet, 7.2 inches (20 meters) in Beijing, China, on August 14, 2011.

FASTEST
Human to Run 5k (3.1 Miles) in Swim Fins While Juggling
32 minutes, 3.77 seconds:

Ashrita Furman

from Queens, New York. He set this record in the Czech Republic on May 30, 2012.

FASTEST
Human to Count to 100 While Doing a Headstand
29.24 seconds:

Joel MacNeil

from New Glasgow, Nova Scotia. He set this record on December 30, 2011.

FASTEST
Dining Set
130 mph:

A dining room table set for six.

Perry Watkins of Buckinghamshire, England, set this record while driving the table, which had been motorized, on a race track.

L789 HO

YOU CAN LOOK IT UP!

The dictionary can be FUN (really)

NOAH WEBSTER

Why do the English and Canadians spell the words "colour" and "favourite" with a "u" while Americans spell those words without it?

Chalk that up to **Noah Webster,** born on a farm in West Hartford, Connecticut, on October 16, 1758.

A few years after graduating from Yale College, Noah became a schoolteacher in Goshen, New York. There he realized that Americans should have their own way of speaking and spelling, different from that of our ancestors in England, and that students needed American textbooks, not British ones. Plus, he wanted spelling and grammar to be as simple as possible.

n 1783, Noah wrote a grammar book that was called the "Blue-backed Speller" (it got this name because the cover was blue). It was the first book to Americanize the spelling of English words such as "colour" and "labour" by dropping the "u." Noah changed other word spellings, too, such as "musick" to "music" and "centre" to "center." The speller was very popular, and updated editions were used in schools for 100 years.

When he was 43, Noah began writing his first dictionary, *A Compendious Dictionary of the English Language*. As part of his research, he traveled to Europe and learned several languages. His goal was to help people to pronounce and use words properly, including new words like "chowder" and "skunk."

Years later, Noah wrote another dictionary, with 70,000 entries— 12,000 more words and about 40,000 more definitions than in any English dictionary that had yet been created.

How Did "Merriam" Get Into the Title?

eorge and **Charles Merriam** operated a printing and book business in Springfield, Massachusetts. Following Noah's death on May 28, 1843, the Merriams hired Noah's son-in-law and son as editors to revise his 1841 dictionary. Six years later, they published the first Merriam-Webster version. It was priced at $6, and sales took off. The company is still in business today in Springfield, and, thanks to Noah, the name "Webster's" has come to mean any American dictionary.

GEORGE MERRIAM

CHARLES MERRIAM

CONTINUED

FUN
FUNAMBULISTS*

☞ **Challenge your family and friends:**

Q Name two words that contain the letter sequence "abc."

A Crabcake and dabchick (meaning a small bird)

Q What is the only common word in English ending in "mt"?

A Dreamt

Name two words that contain every vowel in the alphabet, including "y," in order.

A N S W E R :

Facetiously and abstemiously

MORE

WORDPLAY

A PALINDROME is a word, phrase, or sentence that reads the same forward and backward, such as "eve," "race car," and "Rise to vote, sir." Here are others:

- A nut for a jar of tuna
- I'm a pup, am I?
- Yo, banana boy

A PANGRAM is a sentence that uses all of the letters of the alphabet. A well-known example is "The quick brown fox jumps over the lazy dog." Here are two more:

- Dave unwisely forgot extra bananas; chimpanzees were quick to jeer.
- I humbly request you go wave pixie dust on Jack's fez.

❋ **people who show their mental agility**

An ANAGRAM uses the same letters to form different words or phrases:

- Care = race
- Dormitory = dirty room
- Snooze alarms = alas, no more Zs
- Statue of Liberty = built to stay free

Make a palindrome, pangram, or anagram. Share it with other kids at **Almanac4kids.com/TellUs.**

Can you solve these
FOOD ANAGRAMS?

(Answers below.)

1. **a motto**
2. **a tropic**
3. **cheap**

Can you solve these
SPORTS ANAGRAMS?

(Answers below.)

1. **a wet few ran it right**
2. **lob aloft**
3. **roman hat**

answers to anagram quizzes:
Food: 1. tomato; 2. apricot; 3. peach
Sports: 1. white-water rafting; 2. football; 3. marathon

NEW WORDS

➡ Dictionaries change from year to year. Researchers collect new words with their usage and delete old words.

■ **If a word becomes common, it eventually gets into the dictionary.**

■ **If a word is popular only for a short time or is used by only a small group of people, it doesn't get into the dictionary.**

Beginning in the 1880s, the editors of the *Oxford English Dictionary* maintained a special room called a "scriptorium," which contained 2 tons of pieces of paper with examples of new words that had appeared in print. Today, editors use computers—not bits of paper—to record new words and their sources.

A question guaranteed to stump your friends—and parents!

Q "Constantinople" is a very hard word. Can you spell it?

A "i-t."

Head to Toe!

DID YOU KNOW?

- The average adult has about 5 million body hairs.

- If the average man never trimmed his beard, it would grow to be nearly 30 feet long.

- The human brain contains 400 miles of blood vessels.

- The brain generates up to 25 watts of power while awake—enough to power a light bulb.

- The brain accounts for about 2 percent of an average human's body weight, but it receives 15 to 20 percent of the total blood supply.

- Humans sleep from 5 to 11 hours each night (7.75 hours, on average).

- Earwax protects your eardrum by cleaning out dirt. Each ear canal contains 2,000 glands to manufacture the gunk.

- The eye's retina is about the size of a postage stamp and contains about 130 million light-sensitive cells.

- Most people blink about 15 times in one minute. That's the equivalent of 9 days each year!

- Human eyes can distinguish more than 7 million different colors.

- A human's sense of smell is 10,000 times more sensitive than the sense of taste.

- A yawn lasts about 6 seconds, on average.

- The hardest tissue in the human body is enamel, the outer layer of our teeth.

- Everyone—even an identical twin—has a unique tongue print and set of fingerprints.

- An average human drinks about 16,000 gallons of water in a lifetime.

- Humans and giraffes have the same number of vertebrae in their neck: seven. (Swans have 24 or more.)

- Skin is the largest organ in the body. Adults have about 8 pounds of skin, which, if laid flat, would measure about 22 square feet.

- A human's thinnest skin is on the eyelids, while the thickest is on the soles of the feet.

- Each month, your body makes a whole new layer of skin cells. Every minute, about 30,000 to 40,000 dead skin cells fall off your body. An average human sheds about 40 pounds of dead skin cells in a lifetime.

- Our lungs breathe between 2,100 and 2,200 gallons of air each day.

- A human heart pumps more than 2,000 gallons of blood each day.

- Babies are born with 300 bones, but mature adults have only 206.

- The largest and longest bone in humans is the femur, or thighbone. The smallest bone is called the stapes, located in the ear; it's about one-tenth of an inch long.

- The funnybone isn't a bone; it's a nerve that runs from the elbow to the fingers. The ulnar nerve tingles when bumped against the humerus, the long bone that goes from the elbow to the shoulder.

- A human foot contains 26 bones, 14 of which are in the toes. Each toe has three bones, except for the big toe, which has two.

- Fingernails grow three to four times faster than toenails.

ACKNOWLEDGMENTS

PICTURE CREDITS

ABBREVIATIONS:

GCNY—The Granger Collection, New York

GI—Getty Images

NASA—National Aeronautics and Space Administration

NASA/JPL—National Aeronautics and Space Administration/Jet Propulsion Laboratory

NSF—National Science Foundation

SS—SuperStock

The editors acknowledge Thinkstock, a division of Getty Images, as the source for numerous images that appear in this publication.

Front cover: (Skateboarder) Jorge Alcalde. (Rollercoaster) www.coasterimage.com. (Venus) NASA. (Background) NASA.

Calendar: 10–11: (Center) SS. 11: (Right) Sarah Perreault. 17: (Left) Jean Stoverink. 20: (Left) William Reavell/GI. 27: (Diagram) www.en.origamiclub.com.

Astronomy: 30: Colin Anderson/GI. (Top right) NASA. 31: (Right) William Radcliffe/GI. 32: (Top left) NASA. (Top center) anyjazz65. (Bottom center) Luc Viatourpage. 33: (Top right) NASA/JPL. 35: Stocktrek Images/GI. 36: David Hardy/Science Photo Library. 37: (Top) Harold Sund/GI. 38: (Center) NASA. 39: (Right) NASA. 40: NASA. (Left, top and bottom) NASA. (Top right) Stocktrek Images/GI. 42: (Bottom) Stocktrek Images/GI. 43: (All) NASA.

Weather: 46–47: Kei Uesugi/GI. 47: (Bottom) Karl Shone/GI. 48: NASA. 50: (Top background) NOAA. (Top right) U.S. Air Force, Tech. Sgt. Ryan Labadens. (Bottom center) Queenslander. 51: (Bottom left) NOAA. 52: (Top) www.USDA.gov. (Bottom) NOAA. 53: (Center right, bottom) Juniors/SS. 54: (Top) Martin Barraud/GI. 57: (Right, all) NOAA. (Left, top and bottom) NOAA. 58: (Top left) GCNY. (Center) GCNY. (Bottom) Jameslwoodward. 60–61: (Center) Mike Hollingshead/www.extremeinstability.com. 62–63: (Top) NSF. 62: (Left) U.S. National Guard. 63: (Top right) Dave Pape. 64: (Bottom illustration) NSF. 65: Zina Deretsky/NSF. 66: (Center) Dwight Bohnet/NSF. 67: (Top) Peter Rejcek/NSF. 67: (Illustration) J. Yang/NSF.

Nature: 69: (Photo, top right) www.world66.com. (Photo, right middle) Randy Olson/GI. (Photo, bottom right) Vadim Andrianov. 70: Bandelin-Dacey Studios/MB Artists. 72: (Top) Malcolm. (Third from top) Tom Brakefield. 73: (Bottom left) Uwe Kils GFDL. (Right) Kharadan. 77: (Left, top and bottom) NOAA. (Bottom) Vladislav Gerasimov/www.vladstudio.com. 78: (Bottom) Wildstock/KimballStock. 82: Per Breiehagen/GI. 83: (Top) Arctic-Images/GI. 84: (Center) Cathy Cooper. 85: (Right) University of Arkansas, Division of Agriculture.

In the Garden: 88, 91, 93: (Illustrations) Virginia Allyn/MB Artists. 90: (Top left) Echo/GI. (Top right) age fotostock/SS. (Center right) George Granthan Bain/Library of Congress Prints & Photographs Division. 92: (Bottom) AP Photo/Shawn Patrick Ouellette. 93: (Bottom) John Howard/GI. 94: (Beans, left and right) W. Atlee Burpee & Co. 95–96: (Illustrations) Renée Quintal Daily/MB Artists. 97–99: (Photos) Lindsay Turner. 102: (Top left) Eric Raptosh Photography/GI. (Top right and center all) Lou Eastman, Sarah Perreault. 103: (Top) Dave King/GI. (Center) Eri Morita/GI. (Bottom) Will Heap/GI. 106: (Bottom) TeRoDesigns.com. 108: (Bottom right) Katrina Miller. 109: (Center right) Minden Pictures/SS.

On the Farm: 111: (Top) Exactostock/SS. (Bottom) GK Hart/Vikki Hart/GI. 112: (Top) imagebroker.net/SS. 113: (Bottom) Leslie Town. 116: (Top) GCNY. (Bottom) Nicholas A. Tonelli. 117: Margo Letourneau. 118: (Top) Exactostock/SS. (C) Riccardo Sala/age fotostock/SS. (D, E) Kathleen Brennan/GI. 119: (Bottom) GCNY. 120: (Top) Dave Reede/All Canada Photos/SS. 121: (Top left) Juniors/SS. 122: (Bottom) Fergus Thom/www.goldenspurtle.com. 124: (Top left) Ken Cavanagh/GI. 125: (Top right) Melinda Chan. (Bottom) Ron Kimball/KimballStock. 127: (Bottom) Ron Kimball/KimballStock. 129: (Center) Keisuke Yamada. (Bottom) Sarah Perreault. 130: (Center) Beth Segal/GI. 131: (Top) imagebroker.net/SS. (Center) Adam Cooperstein. (Bottom) Kelly Collins. 132: (Top) Hola Images/GI. (Center) Andrew Barrett. 133: (Top) Snyder's of Hanover.

Fun and Games: 135: (Top) Tali Greener/NorwichBulletin.com. 137: (Center) Julia Fishkin/GI. 138: Stockbroker/SS. 140: Paul T. McMahon/Heartland Images.

Sports: 142–146: (All) Harry Powers. 147: (Top

right) GCNY. 149: (Bottom left) Nantucket Historical Association. 150: (Center) Brunswick Corp. (Bottom) Sean Brubaker/SnowboardArchive.org. 151: (Center) Andrew Short. 153: (Top) Edward Kinsman/GI. 155: (Photos, right) Jeff Salvage/www.racewalk.com.

History: 156: (Center right) Roger D. Hunt Collection, USAMHI. 157: Library of Congress. 158: (Top right) GCNY. (Left top, center, and bottom) GCNY. 160: (Left) Daniel Schwen. 161: (Stamps) The Statue of Liberty–Ellis Island Foundation, Inc. 162: (Top left) Scott Geyer/New York Outrigger. (Top right) Matt Richardson. (Center left) GCNY. (Bottom right) AP Photos/David Goldman. 164: (Center) Abell-Hanger Foundation/Permian Basin Petroleum Museum. 165: (Top) Jonathan Kirn/GI. (Bottom) Jeremy Butler. 167: (Illustration) Kim Kurki. 168: (Bottom left) Herbert Roe. (Bottom right) hoover.archives.gov. 169: (Bottom right) Library of Congress. 170: (Center) American Water Ski Educational Foundation. 171: (Center left) Andrea Booker/FEMA. (Bottom left) Borutstrel. (Center right) www.davecornthwaite.com.

Pets: 172: Cusp/SS. 173: (Top left) Lisette Le Bon/Purestock/SS. (Center) Juniors/SS. (Bottom right) Blend Images/SS. 174: (Bottom) Cincinnati Zoo & Botanical Garden. 175: (Top right) Daderot. (Bottom) Odessa Convention & Visitors Bureau. 176–177: (Center) Ryan Brown Photography. 176: (Top) Susan Engel-Nober. (Bottom) Monica Kissane/www.whitecedarinn.com. 177: (Top left) David Ohmer. (Right) David Herrera.

Useful Things: 178: (Center left) Encyclopaedia Brittanica/UIG/GI. 179: (Top left) Elambeth. (Bottom left) University of Michigan. (Top right) Jazon88. (Center right) www.coasterimage.com. (Bottom right) Bugatti. 180: (Center left) SD Dirk. (Bottom left) Roberta F. (Top right) Jorge Alcalde. (Center right) Odessey. 181: (Top left) JonahLight.com. (Left center) AP Photo/Tomas Junek. (Bottom center) AP Photo/Martin Meissner. 183: (Right, portraits) Merriam-Webster, Inc.

CONTRIBUTORS

Jack Burnett: Be a Weather Watcher, 54. **Alice Cary:** Life at One End of the World, 62; Swamp Things!, 68; Ocean Notions, 74; Rolling in the Oats, 118; Twisted Tales of the World's Oldest Snack, 130; Liberty for All, 158; Float Along the "Big Muddy," 166; You Can Look It Up!, 182; Head to Toe! Did You Know?, 186. **Gregory Danner:** Roach-o-Rama!, 85. **Martha Deeringer:** The Salsa Princesses, 95. **Mare-Anne Jarvela:** Aooooowwwww!, 78; Let's Go Bananas!, 124; Get on Board, 148; Fast Facts, 178. **Martie Majoros:** Turn a Patch Into a Storybook Garden, 88. **Amy Nieskens:** Duck Tales, 110. **Sarah Perreault:** Wet 'n' Wild, 46; The Rundown on Reindeer, 82; Party With the Plants, 100; A Most Unlucky Day, 156; Larger Than Life, 174. **Montana Rogers:** Get Ready, Get Set, Go!, 134. **Jessie Salisbury:** Step Right Up, Kids, to the Greatest Show on Earth!, 142. **Janice Stillman:** Make Every Day Special!, 8; Over the Moon, 30; Our Beautiful But Deadly Sister, 40; How to Tell Time by the Stars, 44; Nature Knows, 53; Weird, Huh?, 60; Hooray for Hummingbirds!, 107; Signs of the Times, 116; Make Way for Camels, 163. **Heidi Stonehill:** Sky Highs, 37; Put Your Best Foot Forward, 152; **Sophia Yin:** How to Feed a Pet Its Food, 172.

Content not cited here is adapted from *The Old Farmer's Almanac* archives or appears in the public domain. Every effort has been made to attribute all material correctly. If any errors have been unwittingly committed, they will be corrected in a future edition.

INDEX